PRAISE FOR JANICE TAYLOR AND

Our Lady of Weight Loss

"Can you lose weight from sheer wackiness? After leafing through Janice Taylor's . . . compendium of dieting revelations and multicolored inspirational collages, you won't want to rule it out."

—*The New York Times*

"More satisfying than a bag of Cool Ranch Doritos."

—*Chicago Sun-Times*

"Many diet and exercise books lack two ingredients: humor and creativity. If those are missing from your current slim-down regimen, seek out *Our Lady of Weight Loss*."

—*Los Angeles Times*

"A fun, irreverent, and wacky read for women who would consider approaching weight loss with a sense of humor in one hand and a rosary in the other. Or perhaps a paintbrush. The kind of diet book Vivi and her pals (from Rebecca Wells's *The Divine Secrets of the Ya-Ya Sisterhood*) would read if they 'let themselves go.'"

—*Fort Worth Star-Telegram*

"In her witty and original approach to weight loss, Janice Taylor encourages us to lighten up, in more ways than one. Offering support, motivation, and forgiveness for our dietary transgressions, Our Lady of Weight Loss gives us much-needed hope. All we need is faith—in ourselves."

—about.com

"The best makeovers begin from the inside out. Positive change comes from positive actions. *Our Lady of Weight Loss* links laughter to self-worth. It makes the phrase 'lighten up' quite literal."

—Julia Cameron, author of *The Artist's Way*

"Finally! A bit of wacky originality, humor, and creativity in the world of weight loss."

—Simon Doonan, author of *Nasty: My and Other Glamorous Varmints*

"A humorous approach . . . Taylor doesn't push a diet plan. She is a weight-loss coach who encourages people to take a fun and creative way to losing weight."

—*Winston-Salem Journal*

"If you are in dire need of a diet starter or just a good kick in the tush, be sure to check out *Our Lady of Weight Loss*."

—*AmNY*

"*Our Lady of Weight Loss* is like a really good motivational dieting coach who could possibly need to be locked up in a mental institution, but you don't care because she is so good."

—fitsugar.com

"Divine intervention at its best and funniest! Who knew? The powers that be are hilarious! Never has losing weight been so much fun!"

—Colette Bouchez, medical writer for the *New York Daily News*

ALL IS FORGIVEN,
MOVE ON

Also by Janice Taylor

Our Lady of Weight Loss: Miraculous and Motivational Musings from the Patron Saint of Permanent Fat Removal

ALL IS FORGIVEN, MOVE ON

Our Lady of Weight Loss's 101 Fat-Burning Steps on Your Way to Sveltesville

Written and Illustrated by

Janice Taylor

VIKING STUDIO

VIKING STUDIO
Published by the Penguin Group
Penguin Group (USA) Inc., 375 Hudson Street, New York, New York 10014, U.S.A. • Penguin Group (Canada), 90 Eglinton Avenue East, Suite 700, Toronto, Ontario, Canada M4P 2Y3 (a division of Pearson Penguin Canada Inc.) • Penguin Books Ltd, 80 Strand, London WC2R 0RL, England • Penguin Ireland, 25 St. Stephen's Green, Dublin 2, Ireland (a division of Penguin Books Ltd) • Penguin Books Australia Ltd, 250 Camberwell Road, Camberwell, Victoria 3124, Australia (a division of Pearson Australia Group Pty Ltd) • Penguin Books India Pvt Ltd, 11 Community Centre, Panchsheel Park, New Delhi – 110 017, India • Penguin Group (NZ), 67 Apollo Drive, Rosedale, North Shore 0632, New Zealand (a division of Pearson New Zealand Ltd) • Penguin Books (South Africa) (Pty) Ltd, 24 Sturdee Avenue, Rosebank, Johannesburg 2196, South Africa

Penguin Books Ltd, Registered Offices: 80 Strand, London WC2R 0RL, England

First published in 2008 by Viking Studio, a member of Penguin Group (USA) Inc.

10 9 8 7 6 5 4 3 2 1

Copyright © Oy-Caramba! Ltd., 2008
All rights reserved

Publisher's Note
Neither the publisher nor the author is engaged in rendering professional advice or services to the individual reader. The ideas, procedures, and suggestions contained in this book are not intended as a substitute for consulting with your physician. All matters regarding your health require medical supervision. Neither the author nor the publisher shall be liable or responsible for any loss or damage allegedly arising from any information or suggestion in this book.

LIBRARY OF CONGRESS CATALOGING IN PUBLICATION DATA

Taylor, Janice, 1953–
All is forgiven, move on / Janice Taylor.
    p.   cm.
ISBN 978-0-14-200524-8
1. Weight loss. I. Title.
RM222.2.T364 2008
613.2'5—dc22   2008001771

Printed in the United States of America

Designed by Chris Welch

Dedicated to my husband, Peter, Lord of the Fries

lord of the fries

and . . .
In memory of my brother, Alan G. Taylor.
This fat-burnin' book is for you, big bro.

FOREWARNED
Be Forewarned! This Is Not a Diet Book

There's no doubt that this book will help you to permanently remove fat (aka lose weight). Nevertheless—be forewarned—this book is not a diet book! There are enough "diet" books out there, including many that agree that diets don't work, so I will not insult your intelligence with yet another diet book. Have you not reached your limit? How many diet books do you need before you realize that it's not the food?!

This book is much more than a diet book. This book is a journey that will help you to change not only your body, but your mind, as well.

Food is not the main course. It is something that is absolutely an integral part of healthy living, but nevertheless it is something that once (lovingly) taken care of can be put in its place and made a part of your everyday activities (e.g., brushing your teeth), affording you the freedom to concentrate on reinvention and utilize healthy foods as fuel for transformation.

Food has energy to it. You now want to eat the healthiest and most positively energized food you can find, knowing that this will propel you forward, allowing you to make the changes you want to make.

Get it? This journey is not about feelings of deprivation; it's not about taking things away from you. It's not even about losing weight (if you lose it, you will find it). Permanent Fat Removal is a happy by-product of transformation.

This book is a road map that leads you to your best self, your higher self, your wise self. It's about YOU and about the person who is underneath those excess layers of weight, who is bustin' to come out. Free yourself now!

Take the Journey.
Move into the "Lite."

ACKNOWLEDGMENTS

Sincere thanks to those who have supported me in so very many ways.

My beloved family—my husband, Peter, my amazing children, Abby, Josh, the best DIL ever, Megan and much appreciated significant other Michael, my mother, Harriet, my father, Ben, and all the rest of the clan: Alan, Larry, Maeve, Daria, Tommy, Jane, Angus, Lesley, David, Nancy, Amy, Peter, George, Gloria, Sue, Jesse, Jill, Dave, and Jeanette.

Platterfuls of thanks to Susan Graves, Jody Graves, Ian Graves, Angela Elsbury, Jay Kriegel, Jim Abernathy, Adam Miller, Matthew Pritchard, Anna Allen, Carol Allen, Carole Goldstein, Pam Roule, Abigail Roule, Wendy Levinson, Dana Levinson, Andrew Levinson, Kate Severin, Steve Bernstein, June Kosloff, Kathy Cano Murillo (www.craftychica.com), Marcella Landres, Diane Patrick, Deborah Drucker, Ron Roth, David Mahl, Ernesto Aguilar, Gina-Fuentes Walker, Sheafe Walker, Reuben Sinha, Evan Mahl, Jeanne McManus, Donna Bellmier, Lisa Morisano, Lucille Conti, Irene Price, Elise Puig, Arlene Parks, Holly Ventura, Maryellen Torres, Maeve Richmond, MaryAnn De Jesus, Anita Gonzales, Olga Kogan, Rob Grader, Gregg Stebben, Kim Gallina, Knoele Babin, Tanya Jones, Janet Rothstein, Patti Iverson, Maxine Siegel, Leslie Jacobs-McIntosh, Lisa Fedich, Versely Rosales, Paige and Jeff Workman, Lindsey Roth-Rosen, Mae Berlingeri, Tina Zaremba, Michael Higgins, Gwynne Philbook, Jennifer Ackerman-Haywood (www.craftsanity.com), Frankie Boyer, Iyna Caruso, Michele Frank, Frances Kuffel (www.franceskuffel.com), Lissa Weinmann, John Loggia, the Our Lady of Weight Loss Choir: Valier, Nikki, Watkins, and Jennifer, Chloe Jo and her GirlieGirl Army (www.chloejo.com), Marney and all my friends at Artella (www.artellawordsandart.com), Cindy Bokma (www.conversations famouswriters.blogspot.com), Jane Weston Wilson, the Time Paradox Group, The Think Tank, Lisa Delaney (www.formerfatgirl.com), Simon Doonan, Kathryn Compton, Kelly Love Johnson, Melissa Walker, Judith Beck, Liesl Schillinger, Steven Leeds, Rachel Hot, and Stephanie Ponder.

Cecilia Knussen, food consultant, Marsha Coleman, professional joke consultant, Kathryn Cunningham, spiritual adviser, Peggy Dyer, personal photographer, Heather Swanson, crafts photographer, Neil Burstein, Esq., Joseph Giardino, and Jessica Millington, Matt and Zeke at fLUID, New York, and Valerie Reiss, Matt Melucci, Holly Rossi, and all my new friends at BeliefNet.com (www.beliefnet.com/ourladyofweightloss.com).

My amazing agent, Debra Goldstein, The Creative Culture. My brilliant editor, Lucia Watson, and all at Viking Studio/Penguin Group who made this a joyous voyage—Megan Newman, Kate Stark, Amanda Tobier, Anne Kosmoski, Molly Brouillette, Jessica Lee, Miriam Rich, Amy Hill, Carla Bolte, and Chris Welch.

A special and heartfelt thanks to Delsa, Kyra, Walter, Gerry, Brain (aka Errol), Denise, and all at the U.S. Post Office, Morningside Station, who cheerfully weigh, measure, and mail my numerous packages. Susan Posen, who one day, many moons ago said, "Thanks for the kick in the tush." And the words stuck like glitter glue . . . and the Kick in the Tush Club was born.

And last but not least, all of *you*—Our Lady of Weight Loss fans and Kick in the Tush Club members and chapters. Thanks for keeping me on my toes and inspiring me!

CONTENTS

Forewarned! • ix

Acknowledgments • x

Introduction • xviii

The *ARE YOU READY* to Hit the *Rocky Road
to Sveltesville* QUIZ • xx

Why Rocky? • xxiii

Hit the Panic Button • xxiv

STEP #1
The Awards Ceremony: Get Ready for
Your Red Carpet Moment • 1

STEP #2
Laugh Yourself Skinny • 3

STEP #3
Forgiveness: A Key Ingredient to
Permanent Fat Removal • 6

FUEL STOP #4
Coffee Meringues • 9

STEP #5
Creative Curves Ahead • 10

STEP #6
Land of the Lost and Found Pounds • 14

STEP #7
Why You Want to Be Fat! • 18

STEP #8
Self-Hypnosis Stew • 20

STEP #9
Sacrifice Your Twinkie • 22

STEP #10
The Rules • 24

STEP #11
A Visit to the Supermarket • 27

STEP #12
The Whole Truthiness and Nothing
but the Truthiness • 31

FUEL STOP #13
Holy & Healthy Apple Crisp • 34

STEP #14
Move Away from Mayo • 35

FASHION STOP #15
Pear-Shaped Baubles • 37

STEP #16
Label Reading 101 • 38

FUEL STOP #17
Pantry Soup from Pat Havlik • 41

STEP #18
Cheatin' Charlie Says He's Going Fishing • 43

VALLEY OF THE CHEERS #19
Go, Fat, Go • 46

STEP #20
Face-to-Face with an Alien! • 47

FASHION STOP #21
Salt and Pepper Earrings • 50

STEP #22
Veggie Vitamins • 54

FUEL STOP #23
Brussels Sprouts à la Janet R. • 56

"E" STOP #24
The "E" Tour • 57

FASHION STOP #25
Tape Measure Belt • 61

VALLEY OF THE CHEERS #26
The Our Lady of Weight-Loss Cheerleaders
Present Go Lite! • 63

STEP #27
On the Scale with Faith and Grace • 64

FUEL STOP #28
Apple & Celery Salad • 67

STEP #29
The Kitchen . . . Friend or Foe? • 68

FUEL STOP #30
Kitchen-Friendly Salmon • 71

STEP #31
The Almighty Altar • 73

STEP #32
Excuses, Excuses • 77

FUEL STOP #33
No Excuses Garlic Chicken • 82

"E" STOP #34
Put On Your Dancing Shoes • 84

VALLEY OF THE CHEERS #35
Melt the Fat Away • 87

Contents

xiii

STEP #36
Do *Not* Try! • 88

FUEL STOP #37
Apple Brown Betty • 91

STEP #38
Kill Your Appetite . . . Now! • 93

STEP #39
Dining Out with Dignity • 95

STEP #40
Sinful Feelings • 99

FUEL STOP #41
Sinfully Delicious Portobello Mushrooms
and Goat Cheese • 101

STEP #42
Afternoon Delight • 103

STEP #43
The Dog Run • 107

FASHION STOP #44
Doggie Wear • 109

STEP #45
The Call of the Cheeto • 110

FUEL STOP #46
The Virgin Mary &
Michelada del David • 113

STEP #47
I'm Eating 9 to 5 • 115

STEP #48
The Clutterless Path • 119

FUEL STOP #49
Pineapple Ice • 121

STEP #50
Counting My Onions • 123

VALLEY OF THE CHEERS #51
Fruity Tootie • 125

STEP #52
Take a Walk on the Mild Side • 126

FUEL STOP #53
Walk on the Mild Side of Pasta • 128

STEP #54
Counting Sheep in the Afternoon • 130

STEP #55
Janny Takes On the Saboteur: Type I • 133

STEP #56
Janny Takes On the Saboteur: Type II • 136

FUEL STOP #57
Janny Stuffs Her Butternut Squash
with Scrumptious Sausage Summarily
(a Tongue Twister
from KITT Club Member, DJ!) • 139

"E" STOP #58
Get Fit for Charity • 141

STEP #59
Dressing Your Table for Success • 144

Contents

xiv

STEP #60
Create a Soft, Safe, and Snug Zone • 146

FUEL STOP #61
Baked Ginger Apples • 148

STEP #62
Ride the Freedom Train • 149

"E" STOP #63
A Golfer's Diet • 153

FUEL STOP #64
Peachy Keen Vintage Cobbler • 155

STEP #65
What's Your Ecumenical Eating Style? • 156

STEP #66
The World Is Your Oyster: Expect the Best • 158

FUEL STOP #67
The World Is Your Oyster and It Comes with a Side of Dill Vinaigrette • 160

STEP #68
Travelin' "Lite" • 163

STEP #69
What a Day for a Daydream! • 165

FUEL STOP #70
The You-Don't-Have-to-Be-Einstein Tuna Casserole • 167

STEP #71
Back in the Saddle Again • 169

STEP #72
How to Get and Stay Jazzed! • 173

FUEL STOP #73
Take a Miracle Dip • 176

STEP #74
Rosie the Ritualist • 178

STEP #75
The Mother of All Mantras • 182

STEP #76
Jammin' to the Beat of Metallica • 185

FUEL STOP #77
Spiced Tea • 188

FASHION STOP #78
Rose-Colored Glasses • 190

STEP #79
Your *Not* to Do List • 191

STEP #80
The Multiplex of Things to Do • 193

"E" STOP #81
Juggle or Jiggle! • 196

STEP #82
Appetite Colors! • 198

FUEL STOP #83
Blue on Blueberry Cobbler • 201

STEP #84
Stopping Mechanism • 204

Contents

STEP #85
Permission to Slip • 207

FASHION STOP #86
Permission Slip • 211

"E" STOP #87
Exercise Your Brain • 213

FUEL STOP #88
How-to-Think-Like-a-String-Bean
Green Beans • 216

STEP #89
Stop! and Smell the Roses • 219

STEP #90
Go Monochromatic! • 221

FASHION STOP #91
Days-of-the-Week Underwear • 225

STEP #92
Emotional Eater • 226

FUEL STOP #93
Rock Star Roasted Fingerling Fries • 228

STEP #94
Your Aura Is Dirty • 230

"E" STOP #95
Hula Hoop Your "Weigh" Thin • 232

FUEL STOP #96
Hawaiian Hula Punch • 234

STEP #97
No Way! You're Not Taking That
Away from Me! • 235

STEP #98
You Have Arrived . . .
Welcome to Sveltesville • 240

FUEL STOP #99
Chocolate Banana Royal Flush • 242

STEP #100
Sveltesville Walk of Fame • 243

VALLEY OF THE CHEERS #101
Sveltesville's National Anthem:
Amazing Weight • 245

About the Author • 247

Answers to Quizzes • 254

Kick in the Tush Club Chapters:
A Miracle • 256

Contents

INTRODUCTION

"It is good to have an end to journey toward; but it is the
journey that matters, in the end."
—*Ursula K. Le Guin*

THAT'S ME ON THE LEFT.

Seven years ago, Our Lady of Weight Loss, patron saint of Permanent Fat Removal, came to my rescue at one of those group meetings where people obsess about food and weight. With a quick twist of my neck, she performed a chiropractic move of mega-magnitude. She snap-crackle-popped my mind into a new place.

She made it absolutely clear that this time was going to be THE time. This time was going to be different from any of the numerous other times that I'd either set out on the weight loss trail and failed or actually succeeded in losing 10, 20, 30, even 40 pounds, but ultimately—there they were! Yup, I found them plus a few extra pounds for "good measure." (Did I find your lost pounds, too?)

✳ NEW POINT OF VIEW

If I lose it, I may find it. For the first time, I get it. Weight loss is passé. Permanent Fat Removal is the goal. ✳

I approached "weight loss" from this fresh angle. My perspective shifted; a paradigm shift occurred. In other words, the tectonic plates in my mind shifted, loosened, and lifted, and a new me came to be.

Our Lady of Weight Loss said, "Weight loss is primarily a mind-set, and while food is an integral part, it's not the main course." (Imagine that!)

Our Lady of Weight Loss continued, "Weight loss can be utilized as a vehicle for transforma-

Caution:
Slippery When Wet

Fat Trail

tion and reinvention." She said that it wasn't just about losing weight and exercise. We were embarking on a holistic happening. In fact, this journey was a spiritual one.

Our Lady of Weight Loss promised me that as I filled my heart with joy, explored happiness and laughter as well as forgiveness, and put some energy into doing the things that I've always wanted to do but never seemed to have the time to do, the excess weight would mysteriously melt off, leaving a fat trail behind me.

As my size decreased, my energy, joy, and spirit—my life—would expand tenfold.

✳ NEW POINT OF VIEW

Food is not the main course. ✳

It didn't take much to transform my form.

a new   identity

sew your own   style

I BELTED MY RED SHIFT and IT TURNED INTO a PaRTy DrEsS!!!

The ARE YOU READY to amble, ramble, stroll, rove, wander, walk, and/or skip on down the Rocky Road to Sveltesville with a smile on your face and melba toast in your bag QUIZ

INSTRUCTIONS: For each statement, circle either "I'm laughin'" or "I'm Cryin'."

1. *I am ready to give up goin' on a bender and promise to use my blender.*
Fruit smoothies for me!
I'm Laughin' / I'm Cryin'

2. *All right already! I am responsible for what I put in my mouth.*
The candy bar didn't fly in on it's own.
I'm Laughin' / I'm Cryin'

3. *"Baked over fried" (or some such equally healthy phrase) is my mantra.*
I'm Laughin' / I'm Cryin'

4. *This is not a pity party. Worse things could happen.*
(I know. This was a tough one for me.)
I'm Laughin' / I'm Cryin'

5. *I will pack up all my sweatpants and donate them to charity (if in good condition), leaving no room for expansion. From now on it's buttons and/or zippers for me!*
I'm Laughin' / I'm Cryin'

6. *Each and every morning, I will look straight into the mirror and tell myself that I can do it! (If you don't believe it, fake it till you make it.)*
I'm Laughin' / I'm Cryin'

7. *I am willing to exchange my "fork-to-mouth exercise" program for another (even if it's as simple as taking a walk, going for a swim, or playing croquet).*
I'm Laughin' / I'm Cryin'

8. *I will do my absolute best to be a beacon of positivity. When that negative voice starts rearing its ugly head, I will not get roped in and pulled under. I will simply smile and tell the voice, "Come back when you can't stay so long."*
I'm Laughin' / I'm Cryin'

9. *I promise to make this Permanent Fat Removal journey fun, even if it kills me.*
I'm Laughin' / I'm Cryin'

10. *Should I have a dietary transgression or two, I will practice self-forgiveness.*
I'm Laughin' / I'm Cryin'

Whether you are laughin' or cryin'—no matter . . . grab your bottle of water (we may hit a dry spot here and there) and let's hit the Rocky Road to Sveltesville!

The journey begins . . . follow the Rocky Road to Sveltesville.

The Town of Sveltesville

Motto
All is forgiven, move on . . .

Mayor
Our Lady of Weight Loss, the patron saint of permanent fat removal.

Medium Weight
Unknown (no scales available)

Official Fat-Burnin' Language
Thinnish

Nature Resources
Possibilities, Enthusiasm, Creativity

Currency
Pounds

WHY ROCKY?

It's understandable that one might ask, "Why am I traveling the Rocky Road to Sveltesville, instead of the Smooth and Easy Path to Sveltesville?"

I'll tell you why!

As you travel your road, you may come across a number of stones, rocks strewn about, pebbles here and there, and some gravel that just happens to shine when the sun smiles down upon it. Ahhh... that's right. The gravel shines, the stones are gems, the rocks are filled with vital information, and the pebbles are precious jewels. Pick each one up as you serendipitously happen across it, and be grateful.

✳ NEW POINT OF VIEW

Rocky Road is not just an ice cream flavor; it's a road paved with gems, jewels, and opportunities for reinvention and transformation. ✳

HIT THE PANIC BUTTON

(for the last time)

At one time or another, we've all experienced what it's like to hit the print button on our keyboard and have nothing happen. And what do we do when the paper doesn't print? We hit that button again and again and again, knowing full well that the paper isn't going to print. Nevertheless, we keep hoping that we won't have to deal with a significant mechanical issue.

I generally hit the print button a minimum of ten times before I'll even check to see if the printer is plugged in. Sometimes the solution is as simple as flipping a switch or adding more paper. The fact that the paper isn't printing doesn't necessarily mean that something is horribly wrong or irrevocably broken, nor does it mean that there's something wrong with me. It doesn't mean that I need to throw out the printer and buy a new one or find some high-priced IT gal to fix it.

We do the exact same thing when it comes to permanent fat removal. We hit the diet button again and again and again. And let's face it—whichever diet button we're hitting—it's not working. It's the same refried, reheated, and repackaged stuff over and over again.

Food isn't the problem. If you follow a reasonable plan, you will lose weight. More than likely either you have chosen a diet that is impossible to live with or your enthusiasm and motivation are waning. You're left dispirited.

You've been approaching weight loss from the same old tired, wrong angle (again and again).

Seven years ago, after a lifetime of yo-yoing, I permanently removed 55 pounds. In this book, I will share my journey with you: all that I learned—my secrets, strategies, recipes, thoughts, jokes, and more—as I traveled the Rocky Road to Sveltesville.

And I promise: It's not the same old, same old. So leave your preconceived notions about what weight loss is or is not and all your attempts and failures at the door. Because this time is THE time. Get ready for a fresh start and a new perspective.

We're heading out on the Rocky Road to Sveltesville. (Wear comfortable shoes!)

"There is a difference between knowing the path and walking the path."
—*Morpheus, from The Matrix, 1999*

❋ NEW POINT OF VIEW

I need not panic. Unless, of course, my elastic-waistband XXXL pants are leaving skid marks! ❋

———————————————————

STEP 1

THE AWARDS CEREMONY
GET READY FOR YOUR RED CARPET MOMENT

Our Lady of Weight Loss

KICK in the TUSH Club

The School of Weight Loss

Upon the nomination of the faculty, the Department of Permanent Fat Removal has conferred upon

_____

a Ph.D. in Dieting

Given under the seal of
Our Lady of Weight Loss
on this _____ day of _____ in the year Two Thousand _____

By: *Our Lady of Weight Loss*

Generally speaking, awards for losing weight—the ubiquitous gold stars and bookmarks for 5-pound losers, magnets for 25-pound losers, charms for 50-pound losers, and certificates for 100-pound losers—are presented to those who attend those group meetings—after they lose weight. (Without naming names, you all know the place I'm talking about, do you not? Most of us have been there, done that more than once. Yes?)

I don't know about you, but I've lost and gained those same 40 or 50 pounds enough times over my lifetime to equal at least ten people. Receiving those awards after I lost weight was fun in the moment, but they didn't help me to keep those unwanted pounds off.

How about we come from a new place this time and change the pattern from the get-go? For goodness' sake, it's like we've got our Ph.D.s in dieting!

We don't need to gain any more. Do we? That's right. Instead of losing and gaining, losing and gaining—the pattern we've been following for decades—let's agree to change our pattern, knowing that we have gained enough now and it's time to reduce. (Hmmm. Wrap your waist around that one.)

Therefore, it gives me great joy to present to you an honorary Doctor of Philosophy from the School of Weight Loss, bestowing upon you a Ph.D. in dieting.

Let the diploma bring a smile to your face and act as a reminder that you are accomplished at knowing how to lose weight. Know that you have gained enough to permanently reduce. This time is YOUR time.

Svelte Talk

DIETER—Something I no longer am. Diets are for losers.
LOSER—Not me. (I get the whole Permanent Fat Removal thing and experience it in Technicolor. Woo hoo!)

❋ NEW POINT OF VIEW

I start my journey on the Road to Sveltesville in a celebratory state, with my Ph.D. in dieting in one hand and a new point of view in the other. ❋

STEP 2

LAUGH YOURSELF SKINNY

I know that 99.9 percent of weight loss programs start with a food plan, but remember—you are blazing a new trail. Let's start with laughter!

HUMOR AND LAUGHTER

"Laughter gives us distance. It allows us to step back from an event, deal with it and then move on."—Bob Newhart

Is there anything more delicious than a side-splitting, hearty belly laugh—complete with tears running down your cheeks? Certainly not! I love to laugh and to smile.

Humor and laughter can help to . . .

- activate the will to live
- lower stress
- elevate mood

- improve brain functioning
- reduce risk of heart disease, strokes, arthritis, and ulcers
- dissolve anger
- burn calories
- exercise muscles

That's right—not only is laughter the best medicine, it gives your diaphragm, abdominal, respiratory, facial, leg, and back muscles a fabulous workout. In fact, a good, hearty laugh burns more calories than several minutes on a rowing machine or exercise bike; and it causes a domino effect of joyous proportions.

Once one sugar cube of joy is set into motion, a number of positive physical effects take place. And without humor, your thought processes are likely to get Krazy Glued to some narrowly focused corner of your brain, leading to increased distress and weight gain.

Laughing at ourselves helps to shed light on our dietary transgressions, proving them not to be the derailing events that we think they are. Humor changes the ways we think and offers a lighter perspective. (Remember, we want to "lighten up" any way we can.)

OUR LADY OF LUMINOUS LAUGHTER'S TOP TEN TIPS GUARANTEED TO ACTIVATE YOUR HUMOR GENE

1. *Look for the everyday humor.* There are all kinds of absurd, silly things going on around you all day long. A friend recently reported seeing a sign outside a local church: "Don't let worries kill you. Let the church help." (Come on—that's funny, and it was right there in front of her!)
2. *Invest in a joke book.* Weave one-liners into your conversation. "I'm not gaining weight; I'm retaining food!"
3. *Get yourself a funny friend or two.* Or better yet, do as my husband did (lucky man) and find yourself a funny partner.
4. *Trade in coffee breaks (or cigarette breaks for sure) for humor breaks.* Tell your boss that in lieu of smoking, you're cultivating your funny side and will henceforth be taking a humor break twice daily. I'm sure he or she will find that very amusing!
5. *New rule: If you hear it—write it.* If someone says something funny, write it down. You can use it later on someone else!
6. *Put a Post-It on your refrigerator, your computer, and your bathroom mirror.* "Have fun." It may take a few weeks before it becomes a habit.
7. *No late-night sadness.* Do not under any circumstances watch the news or read the newspaper or partake in anything that

makes you feel sad or unhappy late at night. It's a sure buzz kill. Sweet dreams require sweet thoughts.

8. *Fake It Till You Make It.* Smile and laugh even if you're feeling miserable. Your brain will pick up on the smile cue and feel better.

9. *Play the HA Game.* There are two ways to play the HA game. You need at least five people, but fifteen is better.

   Here's how you play! All players sit on the floor in a circle. The first person starts the game by looking into the eyes of the person to the left of him/her and saying "ha." That person, in turn, says "ha, ha" to the person to his/her left, and it continues on like this, adding a "ha" with each person. The trick is that you have to do it without laughing or smiling and you must maintain eye contact. And if you make it through one round, you just go on to the next round. It's difficult enough not to laugh, much less keep track of how many "has" you are up to! The last person remaining wins!

   Want more intimacy? The more intimate way of playing HA is to have the first player lie on the floor on his or her back. The next person lies perpendicular to him or her with his or her head on the first person's stomach. And so on and so on until you have a chain of people lying on the floor. Then the game is pretty much the same, except you are just playing for

the Has—the belly laughs from having your head jump up and down. You can't help but create a chain of people cracking up. (No eye contact necessary.)

10. *Hey U.G.L.Y. (Unique Gifted Lovable You),* a not-for-profit organization dedicated to building teenagers' self-esteem, has a laughter CD for sale on its Web site. It's a steal and a scream. Caution: For starters, listen for one minute, then build to a total of ten minutes per day. Wouldn't want you to laugh too much! Visit www.heyugly .org.

Svelte Talk

LAUGHTERCIZING—a new way to happily exercise from Hey U.G.L.Y., guaranteed to tone and burn calories.

UGLY—Unique Gifted Lovable You (whether you are a teenager or not)—nothing unpretty about you!

HUMOR GENE—Believe it or not, something we are all born with. Uncover it, cultivate it, use it, enjoy it or lose it!

❋ NEW POINT OF VIEW

I approach Permanent Fat Removal with a chuckle, laugh, or smile. I am feeding myself and filling up on laughter. ❋

STEP 3

FORGIVENESS: A KEY INGREDIENT TO PERMANENT FAT REMOVAL

"To forgive is to set a prisoner free and discover that the prisoner was you."
—*Lewis B. Smedes*

FORGIVENESS IS A KEY INGREDIENT TO PERMANENT FAT REMOVAL

Many of us have been known to scoff down one piece of cake, beat ourselves up, feel rotten to the core, and then have another slice of the devil's food to soothe. Our fat cells multiply—our pants tighten—we feel even worse—yet we indulge in still another serving of forbidden food, followed by the inevitable platterful of punishment. Results? Broken zippers; broken dreams. (*I confess! My zipper broke on my first date with my husband.*)

In terms of Permanent Fat Removal, holding a grudge against ourselves—being unforgiving for what we perceive to be horrific dietary crimes and misdemeanors—can only impede our progress. There is absolutely no point in unleashing mammoth-sized portions

FORGIVERCIZE
Do the Potato

I'd read about a teacher who asked her students to bring a clear plastic bag and a sack of potatoes to class. For every person the students refused to forgive, they were to write the person's name and the date of the upset on a potato and put it in their plastic bag. The moral of the story was that they were lugging around some pretty hefty amounts of anger that were clogging their spiritual development.

This got me to thinking. Not only am I carrying around a lot of anger at all those other people in my life who clearly haven't read the script I've written for them, but I'm also cartin' around barrelfuls of upset and anger at myself—for my dietary transgressions, lack of exercise, occasional snappishness toward my loved ones, and who knows what else.

Imagine if I dropped a potato in my proverbial plastic bag every time I was upset with myself and dragged it around with me, all day and into the night. Whoa! That's some heavy-duty, weighty bag that is robbing me of my energy, focus, and determination.

Rather than buy bushels of potatoes, I went to the supermarket and bought the biggest baking potato I could find. I baked it, and when it was done, I opened it up and wrote "Sorry" with green peas. I shared it with my husband. He wasn't sure what I was sorry for, but he was appreciative of my creative cooking.

of anger or the relentlessly chastising inner voice upon ourselves.

Confess your dietary sins, forgive yourself, and move on. Remember that one slice of cake does not a fat person make. Get back on the wagon NOW . . . laughing and smiling, if you please!

Here is a forgivercize that will help you to accept yourself with all your wondrous imperfections, as well as lighten your load.

Svelte Talk

FORGIVENESS—A key ingredient to Permanent Fat Removal. You can give yourself absolution or pray to Our Lady of Weight Loss for clemency. Whatever you do, learn from your past and let yourself off the hook now.

✳ NEW POINT OF VIEW

I do not let one "dietary transgression" take me on a ten-year detour! All is forgiven, move on. ✳

All Is
Forgiven,
Move On

7

SIN CITY

🔱 🔱 🔱 🔱 🔱 🔱 🔱 🔱 🔱 🔱 🔱 🔱 🔱 🔱 🔱 🔱

The Devil Made Me Do It!

*I sucked down three Bellini cocktails with the strength of a
Dyson vacuum cleaner.*

Oops, you took a wrong turn!

You are lost in Sin City and the food police have arrested you.

Cash in one of your Get Out of Jail Free cards or do an extra-good job
at vacuuming your floors and carpets this week. Move furniture, sweep
out the hidden dust balls, and move on!

PLEASE NOTE: You are allotted five Get Out of
Jail Free cards to use while reading this book.
Use them wisely or you will be forced to adhere
to the Dietary Indiscretion Court's ruling.

Get Out of Jail Free Card

The Sin City food police
have arrested you.

This card may be kept until
needed. It is nontransferable

All is forgiven, move on

COFFEE MERINGUES

Servings: 24 cookies

Ingredients

4 egg whites
½ cup sugar
¼ teaspoon salt
¼ teaspoon cream of tartar
1½ tablespoons coffee extract
1 tablespoon cocoa powder

Instructions

1. Preheat the oven to 275°F.
2. Using an electric whisk, beat the egg whites with the sugar, salt, cream of tartar, and coffee extract until they hold soft peaks.
3. Drop the cookies by spoonfuls onto a cookie sheet lined with parchment paper. Bake them at 275°F for 45 minutes. Remove them from the cookie sheet and dust them with the cocoa powder.

Nutrition Facts

Serving Size 1 cookie (10g)
Servings Per Container 24

Amount Per Serving

Calories 15	Calories from Fat 0

	% Daily Value*
Total Fat 0g	0%
Saturated Fat 0g	0%
Trans Fat 0g	
Cholesterol 0mg	0%
Sodium 35mg	1%
Total Carbohydrate 3g	1%
Dietary Fiber 0g	0%
Sugars 3g	
Protein 1g	

Vitamin A 0%	•	Vitamin C 0%
Calcium 0%	•	Iron 0%

*Percent Daily Values are based on a 2,000 calorie diet. Your daily values may be higher or lower depending on your calorie needs:

	Calories	2,000	2,500
Total Fat	Less Than	65g	80g
Saturated Fat	Less Than	20g	25g
Cholesterol	Less Than	300mg	300 mg
Sodium	Less Than	2,400mg	2,400mg
Total Carbohydrate		300g	375g
Dietary Fiber		25g	30g

Calories per gram:
Fat 9 • Carbohydrate 4 • Protein 4

STEP 5

CREATIVE CURVES AHEAD

*"Creativity can solve almost any problem. The creative act,
the defeat of habit by originality overcomes everything."*
—*George Lois*

Creativity in weight loss is not limited to writing poems, drawing pictures, hooking rugs, crocheting, singing, or dancing. Yes, you can definitely get lost in arts, crafts, etc., and find them to be very effective tools in weight loss. Heck, I permanently removed 55 pounds while cutting and pasting. (You can't eat when there's glue and glitter on your hands!) But there's a lot more to this creativity thing!

A CREATIVE WRAP

Whether you want to look at your life and excess weight squarely in the face and waist or not, you created them. Hope that's not too harsh. It's the truth. And while you could point the finger of blame at a number of people or circumstances, ultimately, you were the one who put the glazed doughnut in your mouth, chewed, swallowed, and glazed yourself over.

Creative Act of Weight Loss

Wear a bowler while bowling!

So take responsibility and turn a negative spin into a positive spin. The best side of creativity helps us to solve problems, to change behaviors (e.g., from an unhealthy lifestyle to a healthy one), and to entertain ourselves.

TOOLS FOR CREATIVE CHANGE

Imagination, play, and creativity (IPC) are interconnected and are more powerful than three tons of TNT. Just for a moment, let go of the way other people have told you to think, act, and believe. You are your own person. Use your imagination; play a little bit every day—have fun and be creative in the way you approach your day. Shake it up. Walk a new route; chant in the morning. If you're stuck in a rut, light a few sticks of IPC and blast your way out, sending your spirit into a joyful orbit! *(What a ride!)*

Creativity is an essential part of the human experience. It helps us to

- Create balance and order;
- Create a sense of control (and being in control is a major issue in the world of Permanent Fat Removal); and
- Turn a lemon into lemonade (dreadful diet into happy creative experience that is utilized for reinvention and transformation!!!).

Who's creative? You are! Did you put together a dazzling outfit that you're wearing today? Or roast an amazing chicken for dinner? Rearrange the living room furniture? Try a new shade of lipstick? Those are all creative acts that shape your lifestyle. Creativity has to do with imagination.

"Imagination is the highest kite one can fly."
—*Lauren Bacall*

Conditions that foster creativity, include (but are not limited to!):

- Time spent alone. Being alone creates an opportunity to make contact with yourself (your thinner core).

- Daydreaming. It encourages fantasy and reveals new roads for growth. It is a type of trance state—a fantasy that one has while awake—often spontaneous. Daydreams with intention are a form of self-hypnosis. You effectively release all conscious control in the moment and simply allow yourself to go with the flow of your gut feelings or your sixth sense. You go for a mental ride, allowing your unconscious mind to pretend, to imagine. You can easily allow your attention to be directed inward and reach a part of yourself that you cannot reach while conscious or while sleeping. Daydreaming both stimulates the mind and relaxes the body, and it is a process that can help to set goals, manage conflict, boost productivity, increase creativity, achieve goals, and relieve boredom.

WHAT IS A CREATIVE ACT OF WEIGHT LOSS (CAWL)?

A Creative Act of Weight Loss is a time-consuming, brain-expanding, waist-reducing, non-food activity that sends subtle yet powerful Permanent Fat Removal messages to our subconscious minds, thus changing our point of view—forever! Creative Acts of Weight Loss feed our souls and bring smiles to our faces. CAWLs playfully shape our healthy lifestyle.

Did you know that the average adult thinks of three to six alternative ways to sort out any given situation, while the average child thinks of sixty?! So let's wake up the kid in us and come up with sixty new ways to approach weight loss. Whew, sixty? That is a lot. Okay, how about one new way: the way of forgiveness. All is forgiven, move on.

Svelte Talk

CREATIVITY—The quality of being creative. Your choice—you can create fat or fun.

PROBLEM—An unsettling puzzle that invites or stimulates us in a way that helps to bring our creative, fat-burnin' resources into play.

✳ NEW POINT OF VIEW

Weight loss is a creative act. Chew on that! ✳

Nine Tush-Kickin' Creative Acts of Weight Loss *(Guaranteed to Melt Fat) to Help Get You Started!*

Why Nine? In Greek mythology, there were nine muses responsible for creation of the arts by way of inspiration. They were the daughters of Zeus, king of the gods.

1. *Take a hot bath and imagine that the fat cells are melting into the hot water.* Bathtubs are great. When you lie in them, all your fat falls to the side and behind you. It's the only place where my stomach is flat!
2. *Create a pair of invisible goggles that will obstruct your vision when within fifty feet of a bakery!* Yup, they're invisible—the only supply needed is your imagination!
3. *Visit your nearest dog run.* If you don't have a dog, borrow one. It's a great place to meet people!
4. *Grow herbs.* An outdoor garden or an indoor garden. The smell is incredible, and using fresh herbs is a heavenly treat.
5. *Pull weeds.* If you've ever had any kind of garden or yard that was overcome with weeds, you'll know what I mean when I say that pulling weeds is very satisfying. Yank

Janice
Taylor

12

out frustration and anger—it's a good way to get your energy pumping.

6. *Mambo Italiano.* Do the mambo to Rosemary Clooney's rendition. You'll burn calories while dancing, and you'll feel happy, too. Those endorphins will be pumping wildly!

7. *Bowl.* Put a team together! Buy pink jackets and have "The Our Lady Lucky Strikes" embroidered on the back!

8. *Read the menu as if it were a poem.*
   Garlic bread, lightly toasted.
   Chocolate meringue for dessert.
   My tongue licks my lips—clean.
   (Then order "lite.")

9. *Sing.* Loud! Let your frustrations out while you belt out a song.

STEP 6

LAND OF THE LOST AND FOUND POUNDS
(AS TOLD TO ME BY THE GODDESS OF SVELTESVILLE, FIRST COUSIN TO OUR LADY OF WEIGHT LOSS)

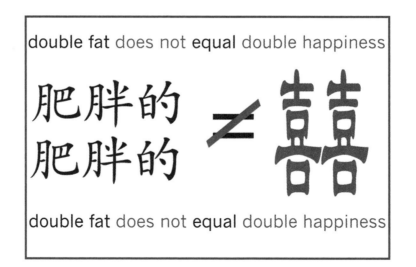

double fat does not **equal** double happiness

肥胖的
肥胖的 ≠ 囍

double fat does not **equal** double happiness

Once upon a time, a chubby young woman was wandering about in the Land of the Lost and Found Pounds, thinking self-deprecating thoughts, when she ran into the Goddess of Sveltesville.

She said, "Hi, Goddess. You are wise, and I am desperate. I want to lose weight once and for all. My triple-XL elastic-waistband pants are tight and leaving skid marks." (She showed her the marks.)

The Goddess asked, "How strong is your desire to permanently remove your excess weight?"

"Hey, are you kidding? Am I not in the

14

Land of the Lost and Found Pounds, and did I not just show you my skid marks?" the chunky young woman replied.

The Goddess calmly continued, "Will you plan your meals, shop for fresh fruit and vegetables, and power walk around the park at least three times a week?"

"Oh, dear," the chubby young woman replied, "I just don't have the time. I'm way too busy during the day, and at night I am way too tired."

"What personal sacrifices will you make to ensure that you will reach your goals?" asked the Goddess.

"Sacrifices?" she answered.

"Until you build your 'want-power' muscles, you will aimlessly move up and down, in and out of the peaks and valleys in the Land of the Lost and Found Pounds," said the Goddess.

Thankfully, the Goddess of Sveltesville then handed the chubby young woman a little pamphlet to read and digest, giving her much food for thought.

THE GODDESS OF SVELTESVILLE'S GUIDE TO BUILDING YOUR WANT-POWER MUSCLES

THINK "I CAN" THOUGHTS.
Repeat after me, "I can. I can. I can." You are starting to feel more confident, aren't you?

STAY CLEAR OF THE NAYSAYERS
You will undoubtedly find those who say, "You'll never make it. It's too hard. How can you live without cake 24/7?" etc., etc., etc.! Don't let the naysayers embed their negative thoughts into your clear mind. Smile and move on, fast.

IF NOT NOW, WHEN?
You have a responsibility to yourself, first and foremost. Tomorrow never comes.

IMAGINE!
Yes, just imagine the level of satisfaction, pride, happiness that you will ultimately experience when you develop positive habits—when you believe in yourself—when you reach your goals.

Svelte Talk

NAYSAYER—He (or she) who mocks your Permanent Fat Removal efforts.
SACRIFICER—She (or he) who gives up nothing real and gains everything in the Land of Permanent Fat Removal.

❈ NEW POINT OF VIEW

Developing my "want-power" muscle will deliver me from the Land of the Lost and Found Pounds to the Land of Sveltesville. ❈

FORGIVERCIZE
The Want-Power Muscle Exercise—Do You Know What You Want?

Sometimes it is easier to know what we don't want rather than what we want. In order for you to build your want-power muscle so that your want power is stronger than Popeye after a can of spinach, try this:

Get in the habit of pausing and asking yourself, before every shopping expedition, television show, meeting, phone call to family member—in other words, before every event or decision—"What do I want?" Would you prefer to buy a black dress or a brown dress? Did you want to make low-fat pizza for dinner tonight or a mammoth chicken salad? Did you want to watch *Weeds* or *Big Love*? From the most mundane to the most serious of decisions, just pause and ask, "What do I want?"

I found this exercise extremely helpful. Almost every pause set off a low-wattage-lightbulb moment. It became clear that I often went to movies that I did not want to go to in order to appease people whom I really didn't want to appease. I ate at restaurants and ordered food that I really did not want, because I did not want to annoy anyone. I stayed places far longer than necessary. Connecting to these a-ha moments shed some light on my underdeveloped want muscle. As these little wants connected to bigger wants, my want muscle grew stronger. I was able to get in touch with my gut feelings—my emotional state as well as the physical sensations that connected to really wanting something. My decision-making process became a lot more fluid and strong, and I began to clearly see what I wanted (as opposed to what I did not want).

Try it! What do you want to do today?

creative **curves** ahead

Test Your Food Vocabulary

As I understand it, the average adult uses about 10,000 to 15,000 of the 30,000 to 50,000 words that they recognize (we're above average, so I suspect we use at least 15,005 words). This may sound like a lot of words to be tossing about, but there are actually about 1 million words in the English language. Some of these words are obscure and make for a fun game.

Match the word to the meaning:

Dibble _____

Groak _____

Gynotikolobomassophile _____

Libberwort _____

Pilgarlic _____

Chanking _____

Farctate _____

Ruminant _____

Lachanophobia _____

A. To drink like a duck, lifting up the head after each sip
B. A bald head that looks like a peeled garlic
C. The state of being overstuffed with food
D. Cud chewer
E. Spat-out foods
F. Fear of vegetables
G. Food or drink that makes one idle and stupid, food of no nutritional value, i.e., junk food!
H. One who likes to nibble on a woman's earlobes
I. To watch people silently while they are eating, hoping they will ask you to join them

(Answers on page 254.)

Source: Canongate.net

All Is
Forgiven,
Move On

17

 STEP 7

WHY YOU WANT TO BE FAT!

HELP! I'M STUCK UNDER A LAYER OF FAT . . . AND I CAN'T GET UP!

IS it possible that your extra layer of fat protects you in some way? Is there a part of you that wants to be fat?

Your unconscious mind and your conscious mind may be at battle. While your conscious mind is telling you (more like screaming at you) that you want to lose weight, get in shape, be fabulous, your unconscious mind is ordering you to eat, and for good reason.

GOOD REASONS TO STAY FAT

The primary objective of your unconscious mind is to protect you, keep you safe. Therefore, if your unconscious mind received any information early on in life that indicates that keeping that layer of fat might protect you, or that eating could take away your pain, it will come forth and tell you to eat. Your unconscious mind has quite a bit of control over your eating behavior.

You may want to keep
your extra layer of fat if you . . .

- fear your sexual energy
- fear being seen (and therefore judged)
- don't like attention
- have very low self-esteem and feel undeserving
- feel that success is for those other lucky folk but not for you
- believe that Permanent Fat Removal may require you to make a major life change (e.g., get a divorce, change jobs)
- fear that you will lose friends

Svelte Talk

UNCONSCIOUS MIND—the holder of your memories, feelings, thoughts, and information that can influence your behavior without you realizing it. Your friend who is doing its best to protect you. No evil force lives within. Just old sound tracks using outmoded information to guide you.

❋ NEW POINT OF VIEW

You are bigger than that bag of chips. Fill in your blank(s) and set yourself free! ❋

FORGIVERCIZE
Exorcise Thyself

Help! I'm stuck under a layer of fat! And I can't get up!

Most of us who have a significant amount of excess weight to remove have invested years and years into being stuck in and under our fat.

Fill in the blank:

I want to be fat because _____.

Make a serious commitment to explore your reasons.

All Is
Forgiven,
Move On

SELF-HYPNOSIS STEW

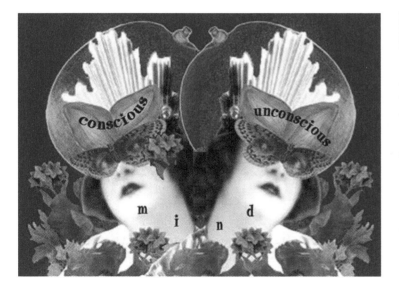

Remember that all patterns in life begin for a reason. Somewhere early on, more than likely between birth and eight years of age, you found that food soothed, relaxed, kept you busy and happy, filled you up, and was your friend. This message was absorbed like a sponge into your unconscious mind and became an unconscious belief. You believe that food equals comfort. You believe that food equals love.

And now, when something upsets you or you find that you are feeling lonely or unhappy, you automatically reach for food, even though your conscious mind tells you not to.

Are you stuck in this pattern now? Do you want to change? One way to start to implement change is to send a new message to your unconscious—a strong message that not only respects how your unconscious mind has been protecting you but is grateful as well. You might say the following words to your unconscious mind.

"Thank you for protecting me and for your good intentions. I understand that you have been doing what you think is best for me. In fact, in your own way, you have been taking care of me. For this I am eternally grateful. I am not exactly sure how this came to be, but I am certain that you had good reason to protect me in this way.

"Nevertheless, I need for those old reasons, patterns, and beliefs to be left in the past, where they belong. I now need to formulate a new pattern for my present and future. Please, help me to move forward, while leaving the past safely in the past— where it belongs. The responsibilities of these old behaviors are now finished."

Svelte Talk

PATTERN—A standard way of behaving that should be examined, tweaked, tugged, pulled, yanked, and updated.

❋ NEW POINT OF VIEW

My unconscious loves me and is doing a bang-up job of protecting me. Now that I understand this, I see that no battle ensues within; rather, a lack of communication. I now can communicate with my unconscious mind and say "thank you for your love and protection." Here's what I need now. . . . (You fill in the blank!) ❋

FORGIVERCIZE
Self-Hypnosis Soliloquy

Repeat the above phrase (or write a new one) to yourself a number of times during the day. Or even record it and download it onto your iPod, allowing you to quietly and privately listen to your own voice sending this very important message to your unconscious mind.

This is a form of self-hypnosis. You are more than capable of setting your mind, making the adjustments that need to be made so that you can now make wise food choices.

STEP 9

SACRIFICE YOUR TWINKIE

"Nothing arouses more hope than the first four hours of a diet."
—Marsha Coleman

NOW let's talk food! Specifically, the devil's food.

If the devil's food knows your name and calls out to you, teasing you and tempting you, and you feel compelled to answer it, touch it, lick it, or nibble on it, best get rid of it NOW!

I realize that this may be a jarring thought. Perhaps your relationship with cake has been your most successful and long-standing relationship to date, and you are reluctant to give it up. Permit me to assure you that you will survive. While separation anxiety can be painful, it will pass, allowing you to go into the "lite."

Keeping your home clear of these items—in essence, making your home a safe haven—affords you an opportunity to establish healthy, solid habits. It is essential that you create an environment that supports your Permanent Fat Removal efforts, a place where you are as free as possible from excessive food thoughts.

sacrifice your twinkie

a wafer thin
thought from
our lady
of
weight loss

Now, give the Twinkie, the devil's food, or that chocolate bar that you have hidden in the back of your refrigerator to your neighbor or doorman, or donate it to your local church, or ship it overseas.

Svelte Talk

SAFE HAVEN—A place free of fatty thoughts and fatty foods. **DONATIONS—**A way of giving away the devil's food while accruing good karma points.

❉ NEW POINT OF VIEW

My home is a safe haven, a place of calm—a place free of the devil's food. ❉

THE RULES

NOW that you have cleared the pantry of the devil's food, you might consider establishing the Rules of the House. Yes, we have to be our own good parent, and in so doing, we must set up some guidelines, some rules to follow.

Here are a few of my rules. Use them as a guideline.

NO SEAT, NO EAT

There will be no standing up/chowing down over the kitchen sink. Set the table, sit down, and enjoy your meal.

KITCHEN CLOSED

I shut down the kitchen and padlock the fridge at 9:20 P.M. every night. It's not about late-night eating. It's about putting an end to the topic for the day. Post 9:20 P.M., I have no food thoughts.

kitchen • is closed

NO FOOD ZONE

I have designated areas in my home that I do not eat in: my office and my bedroom (and of course, the bathroom). It eliminates crumbs in the bed and messy keyboards, and no-food zones train my mind to think of other things while in these rooms.

Svelte Talk

THE RULES—A way of creating order and being your own good mother (not how to find a soul mate).

THE ZONE—A food-free place.

✳ NEW POINT OF VIEW

I make the rules. I create my reality. I am in control. I get it! ✳

FORGIVERCIZE
Your Rules

Make up your own rules! Remember, as we create our own realities, we can create our own rules.

List a minimum of three new rules that may appear small in content but deliver big!

A VISIT TO THE SUPERMARKET

50 ways to lose your blubber . . .

NOW that you've sacrificed your Twinkies, let's get the food out of the way.

Please, allow me to repeat myself! As mentioned earlier, food is not the main course. Nevertheless, it is something we want to put into its place early on, so that we are free to fly. You want to fly, yes? You want to stop the negative chatter and move into your truth, your "lite," do you not?

So let's go shopping for some healthy foods with en-"lite"-ened thoughts in mind. You are NOT stocking your fridge for weight loss. You are stocking your cabinets for reinvention. Each carrot you eat brings you that much closer to your true, glorious, uncovered, uncluttered, authentic, and realized self.

Here follow some tips that may sound familiar to some, so consider this a refresher course; and for those of you who are new to the Permanent Fat Removal game, heed my warning:

NEVER, EVER go food shopping on an empty stomach.

Even though I know better, I hit the supermarket aisles in a ravenous, crazed state one day and downed an entire economy-size jar of green olives stuffed with almonds before I hit the checkout lane.

First some tips and then the food list! N.O.S.S.A. (like NASA, but not):

- NEVER, EVER go food shopping on an empty stomach. Grab a piece of fruit.

- ONLY purchase what is on your shopping list.

- SHOP the outer aisles, where the real food is displayed. Processed foods tend to be in the middle aisles.

- STEER CLEAR of the candy aisle! (Duh!)

- AT CHECKOUT, take a good look at all the healthy items in your cart and feel proud. Take a moment to realize that you are not denying yourself anything; you are not giving up anything; you are giving yourself health.

THE OUR LADY OF WEIGHT LOSS HEALTHY, HEARTY, AND NOURISHING SHOPPING LIST

Dairy

Fat-free cream (for your coffee)
Light or fat-free cream cheese
Light or sugar-free yogurt
Low-fat or fat-free cottage cheese
1% or skim milk
Part-skim or low-fat cheese
Trans-free margarine

Protein

Chicken cutlets
Eggs or Egg Beaters
Extra-lean beef
Lean roast beef
Lean turkey
Low-fat ham
Salmon
Sardines in mustard (the empty containers make great little gardens)
Skinless chicken
Tofu
Tuna in water
Veggie burgers

Grains, Cereals, & Other Starches
(for more wholeness, see
The Whole Truthiness, page 31)

Barley
Beans
Bran flakes cereal
Brown rice
Kasha
Kashi cereal
Light whole-wheat English muffins (yes,
    they actually exist!)
Low-fat pancakes
Oatmeal
Rice cakes
Sweet potato
Whole potato
Whole-wheat bread
Whole-wheat waffles

Condiments

Ketchup
Low-sodium soy sauce
Mustard
Olive oil
Vinegar

Seasonings & Spices

Go crazy . . .

Fruits & Vegetables

Apples
Avocados
Baby carrots
Bananas
Broccoli
Kiwis
Lettuce (all kinds; even in the bag)
Mangoes
Papayas
Pears
Peppers

Beverages

Coffee (can you function without it?)
Decaffeinated tea
Flavored seltzer
Water and some more water

 Svelte Talk **LEAN BEAN**—A healthier, juicier version of a string bean (as in "she's a string bean"; what we aspire to be—lean but not stringy.

❋ NEW POINT OF VIEW

I feed my heart, soul, and body with a bounty of healthy foods that fill me with super-transformative powers. ❋

SIN CITY

ψ ψ ψ ψ ψ ψ ψ ψ ψ ψ ψ ψ ψ ψ ψ

The Devil Made Me Do It!

*While cruisin' the supermarket aisles, I came across a nifty new product
(or just new to me)—peanut butter in tubes. "Great for the kids,"
I thought, "no glass to break." So I purchased a few cartons.*

Only thing is, I don't have any kids.

YOU are lost in Sin City and the food police have arrested you.

Cash in one of your Get Out of Jail Free cards or walk up and down your block (or up and down the stairs in your apartment building) visiting the homes of people who have children and giving away peanut-butter-tube gifts! You can put bows on them if you like.

Get Out of Jail Free Card

The Sin City food police
have arrested you.

This card may be kept until
needed. It is nontransferable

All is forgiven, move on

STEP 12

THE WHOLE TRUTHINESS AND NOTHING BUT THE TRUTHINESS

"Cheerios are donut seeds."
—*author unknown*

Every time someone mentions whole grains, I start thinking of doughnut holes. Truthfully, I find the "whole" thing baffling. No need to further confuse me with a lengthy explanation—a simple shopping list accompanied by a few easy recipes would take care of the whole matter.

THE HOLY WHOLE

There are doughnut holes, which you can find smack center in a whole dougnut, and then there are doughnut holes, which are really small balls with no holes. And yes, then there are whole foods.

Simply put, all grains start off as whole grains, until we refine them. Whole grains are the entire seed of a plant. This seed (aka kernel) is composed of three parts: the bran, the germ, and the endosperm.

Refining generally strips away the bran and the germ, leaving just the endosperm. Twenty-five percent of a grain's protein is thereby lost, and no less than seventeen key nutrients.

Health professionals suggest that we consume at least half of our grains as whole grains (three to five servings per day). Yet whole grains are hard to come by and currently make up only 10 percent to 15 percent of grains on supermarket shelves. In addition, some products that are labeled "whole" have simply had minuscule amounts of whole grain added to them and are not, in fact, whole grains.

How to add whole grains to your food plan

Bake with whole-wheat flour.
Use whole cornmeal for corn breads, muffins, and cakes.
Add bulgur, wild rice, brown rice, cooked wheat, or rye berries to your favorite soups
Whip up ricelike dishes (risotto, pilaf) with barley, brown rice, bulgur, millet, quinoa, or sorghum.
Mix up some whole-grain salads.
Substitute whole-grain pasta for regular pasta.

Whole-grain shopping list
(cross-check with the above shopping list)

Barley
Brown rice
Bulgur
Cereals that are made from kasha, spelt, or Kamut
Kasha
Millet
Oatmeal
Popcorn
Quinoa
Rye berries
Semolina
Sorghum
Whole corn meal
Whole-grain pasta
Whole-grain pita bread
Whole-wheat flour
Wild rice

Svelte Talk

WHOLE FOODS—Foods that are neither wounded nor impaired, but rather have restorative and healing powers.

 NEW POINT OF VIEW

I am wholly holy or holy wholly. Either way, I am whole. ✷

---

creative curves ahead

The word "whole" got me to thinking about wholeness and completion, and that finishing things was a good idea. If you start something, do the entire job.

Read the WHOLE book.

Feed your WHOLE self (including your soul).

Clean your WHOLE house.

Tell the WHOLE truth.

HOLY & HEALTHY APPLE CRISP

SERVINGS: 1

INGREDIENTS

1 pear, peeled, cored, and sliced
1 tablespoon brown or raw sugar
2 tablespoons quick-cooking oats
2 tablespoons whole-wheat flour
¼ teaspoon ground cinnamon
1 teaspoon flaxseeds
1½ teaspoons reduced-fat margarine, softened

INSTRUCTIONS

1. Preheat the oven to 375°F
2. Place the sliced pear in a small baking dish.
3. In a small bowl, combine the sugar, oats, flour, cinnamon, flax-seeds, and margarine.
4. Sprinkle the mixture over the fruit and bake it in the oven for 15 minutes or until the fruit is tender and the crumb mixture is golden brown.

Nutrition Facts		
Serving Size (211g)		
Servings Per Container 1		
Amount Per Serving		
Calories 270	Calories from Fat 50	
		% Daily Value*
Total Fat 6g		**9%**
Saturated Fat 2g		**10%**
Trans Fat 0g		
Cholesterol 10mg		**3%**
Sodium 40mg		**2%**
Total Carbohydrate 54g		**18%**
Dietary Fiber 8g		**32%**
Sugars 26g		
Protein 6g		
Vitamin A 6%	•	Vitamin C 10%
Calcium 4%	•	Iron 8%

*Percent Daily Values are based on a 2,000 calorie diet. Your daily values may be higher or lower depending on your calorie needs:

		Calories	2,000	2,500
Total Fat	Less Than		65g	80g
Saturated Fat	Less Than		20g	25g
Cholesterol	Less Than		300mg	300 mg
Sodium	Less Than		2,400mg	2,400mg
Total Carbohydrate			300g	375g
Dietary Fiber			25g	30g

Calories per gram:
Fat 9 • Carbohydrate 4 • Protein 4

STEP 14

MOVE AWAY FROM MAYO

"What did the mayonnaise say to the fridge? Close the door, I'm dressing!"
—*author unknown*

Dip your french fries in mayo, and you've got the makings of a weight-loss tragedy. Yes, mayo is one of my favorites, but again—in moderation. It's always a good idea to plan ahead and seek out alternatives and create a cornucopia of condiments to choose from.

Are you condiment challenged? Condiments are a type of food product that is generally sprinkled, squirted, spread, or artistically placed on food to enhance the flavor and enjoyment of said food.

More often than not, if pressed to name five condiments, we might spurt out mayo, mustard, ketchup, barbecue sauce, and relish.

All valid and acceptable condiments, but wouldn't it be great to cover our 90-calorie veggie burgers with something more than the usual? Something tasty, tart, and light! Take note, my friends. One tablespoon of mayonnaise tips the charts at 100 calories. That's more than your veggie burger! *Move away from mayo, FAST!*

Condiments & Calories Chart

Balsamic vinegar	1 tablespoon	20 calories
Honey mustard	1 tablespoon	20 calories
Horseradish	1 teaspoon	2 calories
Ketchup	1 tablespoon	16 calories
Lemon juice	1 tablespoon	4 calories
Light Mayo	1 tablespoon	45 calories
Mayonnaise	1 tablespoon	110 calories
Olive oil dressing	1 teaspoon	45 calories
Sweet pickle relish	1 tablespoon	21 calories
Yellow mustard	1 tablespoon	15 calories

Svelte Talk

MAYONNAISE—A rich, creamy sauce or dressing made from egg yolks and vegetable oil that makes one's hair shiny. Slather it on and let it sit for ten to fifteen minutes. Rinse completely.
LEMON JUICE—A liquid that removes stains from your clothing.

creative **curves** ahead

For a real kick, visit the Condiment Package Museum: *www.clearfour. com/condiment.* Imagine covering an entire wall in condiment packets! What a great way to decorate your family room!

❋ NEW POINT OF VIEW

Condiments can be used for multiple purposes. ❋

FASHION STOP 15

PEAR-SHAPED BAUBLES

One of the best holiday gifts I've received these past few thin years is the Marc Jacobs yellow pear-shaped watch necklace. It's a lovely piece of jewelry, and it reminds me of my long-gone pear shape, which, as far as pears go, was quite lovely, but for me, not ideal!

Needless to say, pear-shaped jewelry of any kind is acceptable, be it a pear-shaped diamond ring or pear-shaped diamond earrings. But at the end of the day, I do love the pear-shaped watch necklace. I use it to time myself when I go food shopping.

I head to the supermarket armed with my grocery list and watch necklace. I do my best to beat my own record: Get in and out of the supermarket unscathed and in record time.

STEP 16

LABEL READING 101

My husband was following the Our Lady of Weight Loss–approved, low-fat, low-cal, lots-of-laughs lifestyle for a few months and was steadily losing weight until he hit a wall, aka the dreaded plateau. We just couldn't figure out why, because, after all, he is a man, and as we know, men burn fat faster and lose weight faster than women do—and he was laughing a lot (stop #2 on your way to Sveltesville)! So not fair, I have to say—totally annoying. I digress . . .

We were stumped until about half an hour ago. We were in the supermarket shopping together (a joyous experience, although he wrecks my Olympic speed-shopping personal best each and every time), and he was commenting, "Those ramen noodle packages are one of my favorite dinners." He enjoys boiling up a bag or two, adding all kinds of vegetables. With great pride, he added—thinking that I would be duly impressed that he was reading the labels—"each package contains only 180 calories."

I replied, without even looking at the package—because, after all, I am me and I know the calorie count of just about everything—that, yes, ramen noodles are 180 calories per serving. However, there are two servings per package, so he was eating four servings, totaling 720 calories, not two servings totaling 360 calories.

This led to a discussion about 94% fat-free popcorn. I asked, "How many calories do you think are in that bag that you ate at one A.M. last night?" He said, "A hundred calories?" as if it were a question, because his confidence in his knowledge of calories had been shaken a bit. I grabbed the box in the cart and showed him the label, and guess what—it's closer to 250 calories. Now, multiply those numbers times seven days per week and add in the other miscalculations, and it's clear (is it not?) that he didn't hit

a plateau. He hit a miscommunication of mammoth calorie proportions.

While we are talking about labels, I would be remiss not to point out that calories are not the only things we should be considering. Along with checking for the absence of trans fats, please be sure to read the ingredients, and if any of the following items are among the first five, be forewarned: This product is in all likelihood not only not good for you, but quite possibly bad for you.

Sugar
Sugar will produce an insulin surge that rapidly drops the blood sugar level. Within a few hours you are likely to feel hungry and tired. You will crash!

High-fructose corn syrup
The body processes high-fructose corn syrup differently than it does sugar, and this messes

with your stopping mechanism. HFCS stops leptin, a chemical that communicates with your brain, saying "Hi there, brain. The fat has arrived. You can stop eating now."

ENRICHED WHEAT FLOUR (AKA WHITE FLOUR)

News flash: Enriched does not mean it's actually better for you. This flour has been stripped of anything that is worthwhile, and then those who have done the stripping have added a little back into it so it looks okay. Look for labels that say "100 percent whole grain" or "whole grain" flour.

SATURATED FATS

Saturated fats are found primarily in animal products, and at room temperature, they turn solid. Do you want solid fat globbing up your arteries?

HYDROGENATED OIL

Certain oils are hydrogenated in order to increase their shelf life. Again, these oils turn solid at room temperature. More solid stuff to clog, glob, and blob you up. Items that contain hydrogenated are often labeled as "trans fats." Steer clear of trans fats as well!

Svelte Talk

HUSBANDS—Misguided males who annoy us with their fat-burning ability and slow us down in the supermarket.
PLATEAU—A truly good, calm, and peaceful place to reevaluate strategies and rest (no longer a landing for frustration).

❋ NEW POINT OF VIEW

I derive great satisfaction and comfort from reading the labels. Knowledge is power. ❋

PANTRY SOUP FROM PAT HAVLIK

(THANKS, PAT!)

It's important to stop every so often for fuel. Personally, I'm in favor of minimeals. This recipe from Pat Havlik is a keeper! There are plenty of Fuel Stops along the Rocky Road to Sveltesville. There's a bounty of flavorful foods along the way.

SERVINGS: 1

INGREDIENTS

 1 teaspoon canola oil
 1 small leek, finely chopped
 4 fresh mushrooms, sliced
 8 ounces chicken broth
 4 ounces water
 ½ cup bean sprouts
 2 egg whites
 Salt and pepper to taste
 1 tablespoon fresh cilantro, chopped

Nutrition Facts		
Serving Size (572g)		
Servings Per Container 1		
Amount Per Serving		
Calories 190	Calories from Fat 60	
		% Daily Value*
Total Fat 6g		9%
Saturated Fat 0g		0%
Trans Fat 0g		
Cholesterol 0mg		0%
Sodium 1260mg		53%
Total Carbohydrate 24g		8%
Dietary Fiber 4g		16%
Sugars 5g		
Protein 13g		
Vitamin A 30%	•	Vitamin C 30%
Calcium 8%	•	Iron 20%

*Percent Daily Values are based on a 2,000 calorie diet. Your daily values may be higher or lower depending on your calorie needs:

		Calories	2,000	2,500
Total Fat	Less Than		65g	80g
Saturated Fat	Less Than		20g	25g
Cholesterol	Less Than		300mg	300 mg
Sodium	Less Than		2,400mg	2,400mg
Total Carbohydrate			300g	375g
Dietary Fiber			25g	30g

Calories per gram:
Fat 9 • Carbohydrate 4 • Protein 4

41

Instructions

1. Heat a medium saucepan and add the canola oil. Add the leek and mushrooms and cook them until the leeks turn soft.
2. Add the chicken broth and water, followed by the bean sprouts. Bring the mixture to a boil and reduce it to a simmer.
3. With the help of a spoon, swirl the soup and slowly drop the egg whites one at a time into the soup.
4. Season the soup with salt and pepper.
5. Pour the soup into a soup bowl and garnish it with cilantro.

Janice
Taylor

STEP 18

CHEATIN' CHARLIE SAYS HE'S GOING FISHING

"How does a woman know her man is cheating on her? He starts bathing twice a week."
—*author unknown*

I hear a lot about "cheating." No, people aren't calling me up and telling me about their infidelities with regard to their partners *(well, every so often)*, but rather their cheat days! The way y'all beat yourselves up, you'd think you were breaking up families!

I have to tell you, I don't much like the word "cheat." It bothers me. It has such a negative connotation. I wouldn't want to think of myself as a cheater—after all, cheaters never win! So, no—I don't cheat. I do eat a bit more on occasion, but I definitely don't feel bad about it or about myself. I gave that up a long time ago.

CHEATERS NEVER WIN

The whole idea of cheating epitomizes the negative approach we have toward food. Even if we've given ourselves permission to "cheat," we feel guilty—we feel like we are "bad"!

Researchers at the Center for Human Nutrition at the University of Colorado studied the common characteristics of those who are registered with the National Weight Control Registry and have successfully maintained weight loss of more than 30 pounds.

One of the traits the 4,800 individuals shared was "dieting consistency." Fifty-nine percent reported that their eating was the same whether it was a weekday or a weekend, and 45 percent reported that their eating habits were the same whether it was a holiday or not. Watch what you eat between New Year's and Christmas! (Get it?)

The report further indicated that those who did not participate in a "cheat" day were 1.5 times more likely to maintain their weight loss (within a 5-pound range) over a one-year period. (Please note: the researchers used the word "cheat"—not me! I gave it up three paragraphs ago.)

Follow a balanced plan all week long, stay positive, and should your balanced plan happen to include a small piece of cake or a scoop of ice cream here and there, enjoy it.

Svelte Talk

CHEAT DAYS—Special days when you can eat whatever, say whatever, without guilt or fear of fat cells multiplying. Five Cheat Days are allowed throughout the year (like mental health days) for you to take as needed.

❊ NEW POINT OF VIEW

I am not a cheater; I am not bad. In fact, I am good. Very good! ❊

S♆N C♆TY

♆ ♆ ♆ ♆ ♆ ♆ ♆ ♆ ♆ ♆ ♆ ♆ ♆ ♆ ♆

The Devil Made Me Do It!

*I'm trying to keep my enthusiasm up, but
with each pound NOT lost,
my faith in myself is waning.
I've fallen down the rabbit hole, with an economy-sized
bag of chips in hand.*

YOU are lost in Sin City and the food police have arrested you.

Cash in one of your Get Out of Jail Free cards or recommit to yourself NOW. Toss out the chips, light a candle of repentance, and join the Our Lady of Weight Loss Cheerleaders as they shout it out.

Get Out of Jail Free Card

The Sin City food police
have arrested you.

This card may be kept until
needed. It is nontransferable

All is forgiven, move on

GO, FAT, GO

Why the valley? Because we hit our peaks and our valleys, and when in a valley, how better to catapult yourself out than an Our Lady of Weight Loss Cheer? Get your pom-poms ready!

The Our Lady of Weight Loss Cheerleaders present Go, Fat, Go

Let me hear you yell GO
Let me hear you yell GO

GO
GO

Let me hear you yell FAT
Let me hear you yell FAT

FAT
FAT

Go, fat, go . . . now (please)

STEP 20

FACE-TO-FACE WITH AN ALIEN!

"What do you call an overweight ET? An extra cholesterol!"
—*author unknown*

ALIEN OR ADDICT—YOU DECIDE!

I went to visit my friend Lynda the other day and found her sitting in her very large walk-in closet, which functions as both a pantry and a storage space for all those "antiques" (yard sale items!) that she has picked up along the way. (No joke!)

One wall is complete with shelving that holds her Hostess cupcakes (the ones with those little squiggly lines), potato chips, cake mixes, candy, etc. On the other side, leaning against the wall, sits a very beautiful mirror.

She was sitting on the floor in front of the mirror with a candy bar in one hand, a cupcake in the other, and a bag of chips on her lap. "What are you doing?" I asked. "Watching myself get fat," she answered.

We laughed so hard, tears were coming to both our eyes. She wondered aloud, as I led her out of the closet and tossed those cupcakes into

the garbage without her seeing me do so, if she had been taken over by aliens or if she was just an addict!

I assured her that it was aliens!

There was a time when people didn't think that food was addictive. Certainly one does not go through the same kind of withdrawal when kicking cupcakes that one might experience when kicking heroin.

Yet researchers at the National Institute of Drug Abuse have found that there is an overlap in neurocircuitry. The urge to eat may not be as strong as an addiction to drugs or alcohol, but nevertheless, the behavior of food people, aka "foodies," does give credibility to the idea that food addiction exists.

Foodies experience cravings. (Oh boy, do we!) We are preoccupied with food (thinking about the next meal before we finish our breakfast). We are filled with guilt when we do overindulge (Jewish mothers have nothing on us). We use food to anesthetize, soothe, and stuff down our feelings, and some of us are "closet" eaters.

Addiction and obesity are both hereditary and environmental. While it's true that all the women in my family are fat (my grandmother weighed 300 pounds at one point in her life, and my mother was close to 200—oops, sorry, Mom), the food we eat is intentionally packed with fats and sugar to make us want more. The food industry is extremely competitive, and in order to sell their products and make greater profits for their boards of directors, food manufacturers hook us by adding excessive amounts of salt, sugar, and fat to their products, so that we crave more. High-fat and high-sugar foods may trigger the same brain effects as cocaine or heroin! Take heart, though. Cocaine is a far more powerful addiction than food, and there are measures that we can take to break the habit!

WHAT TO DO!

1. *Get rid of it.* I'm going to say it again! Make your home a safe haven. Stock it with only the right stuff. Fruits, vegetables, grains. Healthy foods that you enjoy, but none of that other stuff!

2. *Indulge on the outside.* As soon as we are told not to do something, we do it. So do not tell yourself that you can never lick cake. Lick it here and there, once in a while. But not at home.

3. *Adaptive little creatures.* Our taste buds will adjust to our new way of life, happily! If you eliminate excessive amounts of fats and sugars, your taste buds will scream with delight when you offer up a sweet baked apple. If you keep on with the junk, you'll want even more junk.

4. *Never get ravenous.* If you let your "food" tank get empty, you are more likely to eat fast and crazy. On the other hand, there's no need to eat when you're simply not hungry. Stay conscious and eat when the first signs of hunger appear.

5. *Trigger situations.* Visiting Aunt May may

trigger the craving for double-fudge chocolate cake, because that's what she always made when you were a kid. For me, visiting anyone's grandmother makes me want rock-hard, fatty balls of burgers. (My paternal grandmother was an abysmal cook, but nevertheless, I still crave burnt balls of fat. Go figure!)

Svelte Talk

ALIEN—A being from another planet or another part of the universe who twists our arms and forces us to eat.

✳ NEW POINT OF VIEW

If there are no addictive substances handy, aliens are less likely to visit. ✳

FORGIVERCIZE
A Lick Here and a Nibble There

Be sure to lick cake at least once a week, and take a nibble or two of your husband's salami.

SALT AND PEPPER EARRINGS

was returning from a road trip promoting my first book, and praise be! I was able to land myself a first-class seat for the very first time in my life. (I am a late bloomer. But so much sweeter the taste of a wide, leather seat!)

The seat was wide enough to comfortably fit me, my bag, my books, and a huge bottle of water. I was having the best time. The man next to me, however, was a whiner. He said that other airlines had more legroom, better food, yadda, yadda, kvetch, complain. When dinner was served, he was less than thrilled. I, however, was over-the-top excited, because dinner was served with real dinnerware and a cloth napkin. Within the napkin was an adorable salt and pepper holder—one side salt, the other side pepper. I gleefully turned to my "friend" and said, "Hey, would you give me your salt and pepper? If I had a pair, I could make a great set of earrings." I continued, "What are you going to make with the stuff on your dinner tray?

Are you going to write positive affirmations on your napkin? I have a fabric pen in my bag, if you want to borrow it."

I guess I have a way of saying things—a certain honest naïveté—because he didn't take offense, although he did look at me like I was from another planet. In the end, he laughed, gave me his salt and pepper, and stopped complaining, but he did not take me up on my fabric pen offer.

Here's how to make your own salt and pepper earrings!

SUPPLIES

One first-class ticket anywhere (dinnertime flight)—HA!

Thread
Needle
Two salt/pepper containers
Beads
Earring hooks

INSTRUCTIONS

1. Thread the needle and pull it through the top corner of the salt/pepper packet.
2. String the bead(s) through the needle.
3. Sew back through to the other side.
4. Add another bead on that side, if you like (optional).
5. Pull the thread through the earring hook.
6. Make a knot and cut the thread!

Fruit or Vegetable

Tomato * Veggie or Fruit

Cucumber * Fruit or Veggie

Radishes * Veggie or Fruit

Squash * Fruit or Veggie

Celery * Veggie or Fruit

Green Beans * Fruit or Veggie

Walnuts * Veggie or Fruit

Carrots * Fruit or Veggie

Lettuce * Veggie or Fruit

(Answers on page 254)

Janice
Taylor

52

SIN CITY

🔱 🔱 🔱 🔱 🔱 🔱 🔱 🔱 🔱 🔱 🔱 🔱 🔱 🔱

The Devil Made Me Do It!

After sticking with my food plan all week, I succumbed to Red Robin's barbecue mayonnaise for my fries!

YOU are lost in Sin City and the food police have arrested you.

Cash in one of your Get Out of Jail Free cards or go bird-watching and find a real red robin! (FYI, bird-watching is exercise. A bonus!)

Get Out of Jail Free Card

The Sin City food police have arrested you.

This card may be kept until needed. It is nontransferable

All is forgiven, move on

STEP 22

VEGGIE VITAMINS

Don't turn your nose up at vegetables! They are key to any healthy lifestyle. And lip-smackin' good! There's a lot of water, as well as vitamins and minerals, which keeps our streams moving.

1. Make a vegetable egg white omelet. Sauté some spinach, mushrooms, peppers, onions, any and every vegetable you can get your hands on.
2. Start your meal with a nice green salad. A big one, at that! And remember, the darker the leaves, the more vitamins.
3. Cookin' up your fave soup? Use vegetable broth instead of chicken broth. Delicious!
4. Add shredded carrots, chopped celery, julienned slices of zucchini, and minced onions to tuna or chicken salad.

LIP SMACKIN' GOOD

5. Layer tomatoes on every sandwich possible. And while you're at it, bake up a bunch to accompany your main meal.
6. Keep little baggies filled with baby carrots, slices of yellow and red peppers, and celery sticks on hand in your fridge at all times.

Svelte Talk

SEXY—One who is especially appealing because of the amount of vitamins and minerals she gets from her daily intake of fruits and vegetables. Her eyes sparkle a zucchini green, and her lips turn cherry-tomato red. "She's a mighty sexy girl. Her lips are like tomatoes."

❋ NEW POINT OF VIEW
Vegetables are sexy, and I can be, too! ❋

BRUSSELS SPROUTS
À LA JANET R.

This recipe is from Janet R. Here's what she had to say: "I recently got serious about shedding the extra pounds that came on from two recent moves. However, I realized that in my haste to get through the extra pressure I was forgetting the rule that 'veggies are your really good friend.' So now I'm back in the saddle and wanted to share my favorite veggie recipe with you. FYI, it works just as well with fresh cauliflower."

Bravo, Janet. Thanks for the recipe, and as Our Lady of Weight Loss says, you can let those pounds visit, but you can't let them move back in!

The result is a crunchy, tasty morsel that is low in calories and works great when you must have something crunchy and filling (story of my life!).

INGREDIENTS

Brussels sprouts
Nonstick spray
Olive oil
Soy sauce

INSTRUCTIONS

Preheat the oven to 375–395°F, depending upon how hot yours gets. Wash the brussels sprouts, cut each one in half, and place them on a cookie sheet sprayed with nonstick spray. Sprinkle them with olive oil, and a little soy sauce, and bake them for about 30 minutes.

"E" STOP 24

THE "E" TOUR

EIGHT EXCELLENT STAY-FIT TIPS FOR THE EXERCISE-PHOBIC

My mother recalls, "When you were a baby, I could plop you in the middle of the floor and leave you there for the entire day (not that I did), and you would be in the exact same spot when I returned." Thanks, Mom!

Therefore, for me to love power walking and "weight" lifting is a miracle. How did I bring myself to love the "E" word? I reframed it!

Reframing is a way of looking at something from another angle. I am a master at it, and it is the cornerstone of my entire life. It does not require a hammer or a nail, just a twist of the neck and head—a fresh perspective.

1. *Reframe the "E" word.* If your associations with exercise are painful in any way, call it "movement." I don't think of myself as exercising on a daily basis. I'm simply "taking a

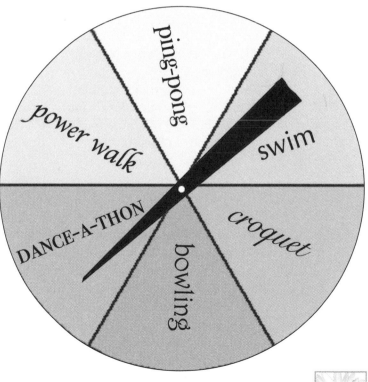

walk" or "lifting" the bags from the super-market while I walk up five flights of stairs.

2. *Find an activity that makes your heart sing.* I know that there is a lot of talk out there about the importance of "getting your heart to pumping," but I say, first let's get our hearts to "singing" (another great reframe).

If you have never set foot in a health club (I am not referring to the spa portion), here follows a list of activities that just might send you away from the kitchen, out your front door, and into the fresh air:

Badminton
Bowling
Croquet
Dancing (alone, with a partner, or in a class)
Ping-Pong
Swimming (and treading water)
Walking for a cause (once you've made a commitment to a cause and have collected money from friends, family, and cowork-ers, it's hard to back out)
(See the chart on page 60 for other possible ways to burn calories and tone up!)

3. *Walk in packs—or at least in twos.* Support in life and in weight loss (every inch of the "weigh") is monumentally important. If you are unlikely to get up and walk without hav-ing someone else to report to, for goodness' sake, find someone to report to, team up with, be accountable to (someone who doesn't get on your last nerve).

4. *This morning's goal.* I know that conven-tional wisdom tells us to set SMART goals (specific, measurable, attainable, reasonable, timely)—but for the exercise-phobic (not the gym bunny) that kind of goal setting might feel overwhelming. So I've created the "wheel of movement" (see above). If you wake and find yourself not in the condition to think, spin the wheel of movement and just do whatever comes up.

5. *Variety—the spice of life.* The wheel of move-ment is helpful in varying your daily routine. Each spin of the wheel is an adventure. Who knows where you'll land or what you'll be doing!

6. *Give yourself a star.* I know that "they" say to keep a journal or chart that indicates your improvement, feelings, and accomplish-ments relating to your "movement" experi-ence. If you are already keeping a daily journal, whether it be your insightful mus-ings or your list of gratitudes, simply add a box to the bottom of the page and for each day that you moved, give yourself a gold star. For each day that you broke a sweat, two stars; and for each day that you were drenched and the endorphins were flying high in the sky, give yourself three stars. At the end of the week, you will easily see if you need to step it up.

7. *Keep exploring and reading about movement.* Reading and thinking burns calories, and perhaps you'll inadvertently find a new kind of movement that further excites you.

8. *And finally, consider this mind-twisting fact.* Do you know how an advanced chess player

trains for a game of chess, one of the most cerebral games there is? By running or swimming, because they know that they must be physically fit to sustain those long periods of mental concentration that a chess tournament requires.

Svelte Talk

MOVEMENT—Exercise in disguise for the exercise-phobic.

※ NEW POINT OF VIEW

I exercise for my body and my mind, not for me. ※

_____

※ NEW POINT OF VIEW

A simple game of bowling can get you moving. Exercise comes in many forms! Think outside the gym! ※

_____

The "E" Word Chart of Nonthreatening Ways to Increase Your Mental Abilities Through Movement

Oh my lady, look at all the fun things you can do to "move."

Activity	Approximate calories burned per hour	Activity	Approximate calories burned per hour
Automobile repair	175	Mowing lawn (general)	325
Badminton (social, general)	265	Music playing (cello, flute, horn)	120
Billiards	150	Music playing (drums)	235
Bowling	175	Music playing (guitar, rock and roll)	175
Carpentry (general)	205	Painting, papering, plastering	265
Child care	205	Pushing child in stroller	150
Cleaning (heavy, vigorous effort)	266	Raking lawn	235
Cleaning (light, moderate effort)	150	Scrubbing floors	325
Cooking or food preparation *(unless eating while you are preparing)*	150	Shoveling snow by hand	355
		Shuffleboard or lawn bowling	175
Croquet	150	Sitting and playing with child(ren)	150
Curling (your hair!)	235	Snorkeling	295
Dancing, ballroom (slow)	175	Snowmobiling	205
Darts, wall or lawn	150	Standing!!!!	100
Electrical work or plumbing	205	Stretching or hatha yoga	235
Fishing from boat (sitting)	150	Sweeping garage or sidewalk	235
Frisbee playing (general)	175	Swimming or treading water	270
Gardening (general)	325	Table tennis or Ping-Pong	235
Golf (carrying clubs)	235	Unicycling	295
Golf, miniature	175	Volleyball (noncompetitive)	175
Horseback riding (walking)	150	Walking (2 mph, slow pace)	145
Hunting (general)	295	Walking (3 mph, with dog)	205
Marching band	235	Walking (carrying 15 lb load)	205
Moving furniture (household)	415		

Source: nutristragtegy.com

I'm accepting applications for the Our Lady of Weight Loss marching band.
What kind of uniform should we design?

TAPE MEASURE BELT

THE MAKE A FASHION STATEMENT... TAPE MEASURE BELT

Speaking of "style," you can be sure that making a tape measure belt will bring out the fashionista in you!

I no longer needed to measure my thighs, waist, or hips in proportion to each other (no, I will never be 36-25-36, and who is?), so I taped my tape measure to a loose belt. Everyone loves it! LOVES it! When you tune into next year's Fashion on Seventh Avenue and you see everyone wearing tape measures all over their bodies, you'll know who started this hot trend! Our Lady of Weight Loss, that's who!

Supplies

Two-sided craft tape
Tape measure (color of your choice)
Very loose-fitting belt!

Instructions

Cut small strips of the two-sided craft tape. Adhere them to back of the tape measure. One section at a time, remove the peel and tape the tape measure to the middle of the belt. It's best to do this in sections, because one long piece of two-sided tape becomes difficult to work with and its sticking power is the same in smaller pieces.

FASHION NOTE ON BELTS

Whether you are making your own belt or buying one (woo hoo, more shopping), I know it's a big moment in Permanent Fat Removal to be able to tuck your belt into your pant loops, but don't limit your thinking to your waist. Remember, this is creative weight loss and you might consider belting up your hips or ribs!

Waist cincher

Take a wide belt to your waist—the thicker the better, square buckled, clunky metal, "diamond"-encrusted—keeping in mind that the visual weight of this accessory is hefty. In other words, no need to bangle up, bead up, or add twenty necklaces. The belt says it all!

Empire waist

Your bust-enhancing, age-reducing empire-waist belt should be kept small, simple, subtle, and sexy. Thin belts in fabulous colors and textures give way to a thin look.

Hip-huggers

This belt brings the eye to our much-beloved curvy hips and creates shape in a different but equally powerful way. Sassy, playful, feisty, hip-huggers are the hippest.

VALLEY 26 OF THE CHEERS

THE OUR LADY OF WEIGHT-LOSS CHEERLEADERS PRESENT GO LITE!

Hey, hey, it's time to go LITE.

Everybody yell IT'S A FAT-FREE FIGHT

IT'S A FAT-FREE FIGHT!

Hey, hey, yell it again

Everybody yell IT'S a FAT-FREE FIGHT!

IT'S A FAT-FREE FIGHT!

Go, fat, fast.

Go, fat, fast.

ON THE SCALE WITH FAITH AND GRACE

"A smiling face is half the meal."
—*Latvian proverb*

My friend Maggie told me that one of two things happens when she gets on the scale. If she's lost weight, she says, "Yeah!" and eats. If she's gained weight, she says, "Why bother?" And eats. Clearly, Maggie should not weigh herself daily; perhaps not even weekly!

WHAT DOES THE SCALE MEASURE?

Do you know what the scale really measures—scientifically, that is? Every object in the universe with mass attracts every other object with mass. (Some more massive than others!) Therefore, there is a pull, a force—an attraction (even better)—between you and the earth.

Your bathroom scale measures that force of attraction, and that force is called your weight! If you look at it in those terms, it takes the emphasis off fat and puts it on gravitational pull.

64

Nowhere in scientific data—that I could find—does it state that the scale measures hideous fat. It is only a number, and I realized that I didn't have to be in a twist over the attraction between the earth and me. After all, I am happy to be considered attractive.

Let's promise here and now that we're not going to get fixated on the numbers. The turtle wins this race, and numbers fluctuate with the wind. Seriously, even the weather can make you retain water!

Nevertheless, statistics show that people who weigh themselves regularly not only lose weight faster, but keep it off longer.

HOW OFTEN SHOULD WE WEIGH IN AND WHAT IS THE BEST WAY TO WEIGH IN?

If you are like me—the kind of person who allows the number on the scale to dictate the mood of the day—then only weigh yourself once a week and on a day when no one is depending upon you in any big way. In other words, do not dispense life advice or operate heavy equipment on weigh-in day.

And remember, only weigh yourself first thing in the morning, after you "relieve" yourself, before coffee, and naked, of course. Every ounce counts.

And for goodness' sake, find the right spot. Tiled floors offer varied readings, depending on the dip of the tile. Take advantage of that dip—find the lowest point, and leave your scale there!

Svelte Talk

SCALE—Device that measures the earth's attraction to us, unlike ancient times, when the scale was used as a torture device. No longer about rejection, it is about acceptance and balance.

❊ NEW POINT OF VIEW

The scale does not measure my self-worth, but rather the attraction the earth has to me! ❊

FORGIVERCIZE
Mesmerizing Measurements

In order to put this number thing into perspective, let's contemplate for a moment or two, all the things that we measure (in addition to our weight).

We measure ingredients for recipes, we measure square feet in our homes, we measure height. We measure levels in blood, urine, and stool samples. We measure sperm counts, cell counts, potassium levels, the amount of fat and sugar pulsating through our veins. We measure BMI, GI, our salaries. What else do we measure?

Make your list of things you measure, and realize that human beings have an intense need to make order out of things. Measuring helps create order. So go ahead.

I invite you to create all the order you need, and once a calm sense of order falls into place, take in a deep breath, exhale without measuring the amount of carbon dioxide you are letting out, and then let go. Let go of the numbers and know that the essence of who you are is immeasurable. You far exceed any number, any standard.

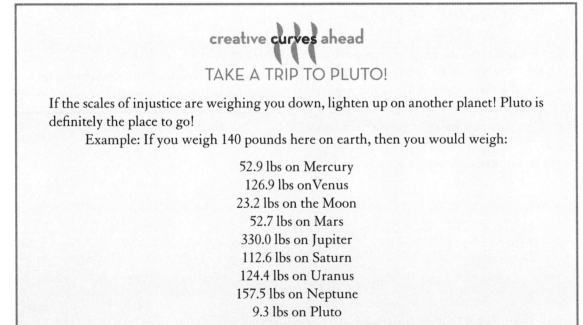

creative curves ahead

TAKE A TRIP TO PLUTO!

If the scales of injustice are weighing you down, lighten up on another planet! Pluto is definitely the place to go!

Example: If you weigh 140 pounds here on earth, then you would weigh:

52.9 lbs on Mercury
126.9 lbs on Venus
23.2 lbs on the Moon
52.7 lbs on Mars
330.0 lbs on Jupiter
112.6 lbs on Saturn
124.4 lbs on Uranus
157.5 lbs on Neptune
9.3 lbs on Pluto

Source: http://www.exploratorium.edu/ronh/weight/index.html

APPLE & CELERY SALAD
(AKA POMME ET CÉLERI SALADE)

As long as we are obsessing about the scale (we are, aren't we?), we may as well whip up a simple salad that contains "negative calorie" foods. Theoretically, negative calorie foods are those that contain fewer calories than we expend chewing them. Sounds like exercise to me!

SERVING: 1

INGREDIENTS

   1 cup apple, peeled and cut into little cubes (tart ones are best; I prefer Granny Smith apples)
   Juice from one fresh lemon
   1 cup celery, cut into similar bite-sized cubes
   2 tablespoons reduced-calorie French dressing

INSTRUCTIONS

Mix the apple with the lemon juice first (so the apple doesn't discolor). Then add the rest!

Nutrition Facts		
Serving Size (327g)		
Servings Per Container 1		
Amount Per Serving		
Calories 150	Calories from Fat 40	
		% Daily Value*
Total Fat 4.5g		7%
Saturated Fat 0.5g		3%
Trans Fat 0g		
Cholesterol 0mg		0%
Sodium 420mg		18%
Total Carbohydrate 33g		11%
Dietary Fiber 4g		16%
Sugars 24g		
Protein 1g		
Vitamin A 15%	•	Vitamin C 50%
Calcium 6%	•	Iron 2%

*Percent Daily Values are based on a 2,000 calorie diet. Your daily values may be higher or lower depending on your calorie needs:

	Calories	2,000	2,500
Total Fat	Less Than	65g	80g
Saturated Fat	Less Than	20g	25g
Cholesterol	Less Than	300mg	300 mg
Sodium	Less Than	2,400mg	2,400mg
Total Carbohydrate		300g	375g
Dietary Fiber		25g	30g

Calories per gram:
Fat 9 • Carbohydrate 4 • Protein 4

STEP 29

THE KITCHEN . . . FRIEND OR FOE?

Come on baby, light my fire.

After I permanently removed 55 pounds, I realized that I had an ambivalent relationship with my kitchen.

I'd spent decades foraging through the refrigerator, eating in an unhealthful manner—creating all kinds of ill feelings and ill health. Even though the kitchen is home to many sacred fruits, vegetables, and whole grains, it still holds old memories of overeating and loss of control.

However, when I realized the power the kitchen generates and that the kitchen is the center of our well-being, I just had to align myself with it. It's not just about the food that is in it, it's also about the energy that emanates from it.

Is not the kitchen the place where people congregate, no matter what is going on in other rooms? When you have a party, people gravitate to the kitchen.

KITCHEN POWER

According to the laws of feng shui, the kitchen is where we connect with the energies that nourish us. These energies are not limited to the physical—they are also financial energies (e.g., money) and emotional energies (e.g., your family). The kitchen is not just a place to store the groceries or dish up delightful dinners, but also a place to connect with ourselves and others and to receive blessings and feel gratitude for all the nourishment, riches, and love that we have in our lives in emotional, physical, and spiritual ways.

Therefore, the cleaner, warmer, and more welcoming your kitchen, the more likely you are to thrive on all levels. Got to get that feng shui energy a-flowin' and a-glowin'!

THE STOVE REPRESENTS YOUR POTENTIAL
The more often you use your stove, the easier it will be create health, wealth, and romance in your life. (I am so in trouble.)

FRUIT REPRESENTS VITALITY AND HEALTH
Nourishing vibes fill the air. Always have a big, colorful bowl on your counter with fresh fruits available for yourself and your guests.

KEEP YOUR KITCHEN COUNTERS AS CLEAR AS POSSIBLE
Other than the lovely and powerful bowl of fruit that we just spoke about, clear your counters—find a storage place for all those appliances that you don't use on a daily basis.

KITCHEN CLUTTER MAY WELL TRANSLATE INTO EXCESS WEIGHT, so you certainly want to keep your cabinets and drawers organized. It is okay to have one "junk" drawer—a place to keep your odds 'n' ends, like batteries, keys, Scotch tape—as long as you can easily close the drawer. Again, it is important to keep the energy flowing! Steer clear of energy traps!

KNIVES AND SCISSORS SHOULD BE KEPT EITHER IN A DRAWER OR IN A WOODEN KNIFE BLOCK
Their cutting edges cut energy and create conflict and anxiety.

DO NOT STORE HEAVY OR BULKY ITEMS OVERHEAD
Having these things overhead can make you feel feelings of overwhelmed. If your pots and pans are kept in an overhead rack, make sure it is nowhere near where you stand to chop, dice, cook, or clean. Get it?

Svelte Talk

KITCHEN—A room or part of a room or building where love, prosperity, and health are cooked up, dished out, and shared.

❋ NEW POINT OF VIEW

The kitchen generates love and support. It is a place where platters full of opportunity are cooked up and sent sailing out into the universe, like no other room in the house. ❋

creative **curves** ahead

For an extra-curvy kick in the tush regarding your weight-loss efforts, put a mirror on the refrigerator. Be sure to smile at yourself each time you pass it. Send love vibes and remember to forget to eat (in an excessive, unhealthful manner, that is).

KITCHEN-FRIENDLY SALMON

SERVINGS: 4

INGREDIENTS

4 salmon fillets (6 ounces each)
¼ teaspoon kosher salt
1 teaspoon lemon pepper seasoning
2 teaspoons vegetable or olive oil
2 tablespoons capers
½ cup fat-free sour cream
1 tablespoon lemon juice
Zest from one lemon
1 tablespoon Parmesan cheese
1 tablespoon plus 1 teaspoon finely chopped chives
¼ teaspoon ground pepper

INSTRUCTIONS

1. Preheat the oven to 400°F.
2. Season the salmon fillets with the salt and lemon pepper seasoning.
3. Over medium heat, preheat an ovenproof, nonstick skillet. Add the oil. Once it is heated, add the salmon fillets skin side down.

Nutrition Facts		
Serving Size (226g)		
Servings Per Container 4		
Amount Per Serving		
Calories 380	Calories from Fat 150	
		% Daily Value*
Total Fat 17g		**26%**
Saturated Fat 2.5g		**13%**
Trans Fat 0g		
Cholesterol 125mg		**42%**
Sodium 1120mg		**47%**
Total Carbohydrate 7g		**2%**
Dietary Fiber 1g		**4%**
Sugars 2g		
Protein 46g		
Vitamin A 6%	•	Vitamin C 10%
Calcium 10%	•	Iron 10%

*Percent Daily Values are based on a 2,000 calorie diet. Your daily values may be higher or lower depending on your calorie needs:

	Calories	2,000	2,500
Total Fat	Less Than	65g	80g
Saturated Fat	Less Than	20g	25g
Cholesterol	Less Than	300mg	300 mg
Sodium	Less Than	2,400mg	2,400mg
Total Carbohydrate		300g	375g
Dietary Fiber		25g	30g

Calories per gram:
Fat 9 • Carbohydrate 4 • Protein 4

Cook for 3–4 minutes and add the capers to the pan. Do not turn the fish over!

4. Immediately place the fish in the oven (still not turned over), and let it cook in the oven for 10–12 minutes.

5. In the meantime, make the sauce: In a small bowl, combine the sour cream, lemon juice, zest, Parmesan cheese, and 1 tablespoon of the chives. Season the sauce with salt and pepper. Set it aside.

6. After the fish is done, remove it from the oven and turn it over onto a plate. Serve it with the sauce and garnish it with the remaining chives. Delicious!

THE ALMIGHTY ALTAR

"I eat merely to put food out of my mind."
—N. F. Simpson

BUILD IT, AND YE SHALL LOSE!

Constructing an altar is essential for a number of reasons

It signifies your intention to slim down while you laugh it up in stone, macaroni, or dried beans, depending upon your building materials.

It creates a space that encourages tranquility and peace, a space of calm where emotional eating simply does not exist.

It connects us to the many aspects of a role that has played a major part in our lives: "the dieter," or "the fat one."

We now have an opportunity to reflect upon this role and change it, tweak it, accept it.

An altar is designed to bring about changes in our growth, girth, attitude, circumstances, and circumference. It connects the way we were to who we wish to be.

And finally, it is a place to pay homage to

Our Lady of Weight Loss, the patron saint of Permanent Fat Removal. (Why not? She deserves it!)

WHERE WILL YOU PLACE YOUR WEIGHT-LOSS ALTAR?

Before we begin construction, we need to figure out where we will place our altars. Here are some things to consider.

Do you want your altar to be in a private, quiet area of your home, or someplace where it will be seen by all? If you place your altar in a more public place within your home, you run the risk of friends and family touching your altar, rearranging your candles, and making comments. Will this annoy you (I'm speaking from experience)? If so, place it in the far corner of the least visited room (maybe the master bath).

If you are going to display candles or incense on your altar, or any other burning materials, please be sure to place it far from drapes, children, and pets! Dresser tops make most excellent bases for altars, as do shelves and windowsills. And, of course, a stand in the corner of the room is always a lovely choice. Think outside the box (as in outside of your four walls)—create an altar in your garden.

THE ALTAR ITSELF

Although not mandatory, altar cloths do add color and texture and help to set the mood. And they provide another opportunity to be creative. You don't have to buy an altar cloth. You can use doilies, scarves, or old linens. Always good to use something that has meaning to you.

You might want to give some thought to the color of your altar. This was a complicated decision for me. Although we are talking about weight loss here, for me weight loss is a vehicle for reinvention and transformation. It's as much about love, energy, health, spirit, creativity, self-control, and rebirth as about actual pounds permanently removed. This means that any and all colors work.

Try pink for love; red for energy, health, and strength; purple for spiritual matters; blue for healing, tranquility, and health; orange for creativity and encouragement; black for self-control and rebirth.

WHAT WILL YOU PUT ON YOUR ALTAR?

The objects you decide to place on your altar are entirely up to you. The altar is a tool that connects your conscious mind to your unconscious mind and sets your intention. As long as the items on your altar make sense to you, resonate with you, they are fine. You might consider including photos, statues, written words, poems, recipes, plants, cards, stones, books, coins, and perhaps a Twinkie or two—in their wrappers, of course! No tasting.

Svelte Talk

TWINKIE—Sacrificial offering to the patron saint of Permanent Fat Removal, proving deep devotion and commitment to the Permanent Fat Removal process.

REBIRTH—The revival of important parts of myself that have been buried under excess layers of adipose tissue.

❋ NEW POINT OF VIEW

My altar serves to connect me to my intention to be the best that I can be. ❋

SIN CITY

The Devil Made Me Do It!

*My car seat suggests that there may be some unconscious,
on-the-run speed-eating going on here.
Crumbs everywhere.*

Oops, you took a wrong turn!

You are lost in Sin City. You have committed a misdemeanor of unconscious proportions. The food police have arrested you.

Cash in one of your Get Out of Jail Free cards or walk an extra fifteen hundred steps per day daily (in addition to the ten thousand steps I assume you are already walking!) for one week.

Get Out of Jail Free Card

The Sin City food police
have arrested you.

This card may be kept until
needed. It is nontransferable

All is forgiven, move on

STEP 32

EXCUSES, EXCUSES

"If you don't want to do something, one excuse is as good as another."
—*Yiddish proverb*

Keeping in mind that there are reasons and then there are excuses, and that what may be a valid reason for one person may be an excuse for another, tell me . . . what's your excuse? Believe me, I have heard them all! Heck, I've used them all!

Bad haircut is my own personal favorite. Listen, I can take a lot in life—really! But a bad haircut is enough to throw me over the edge. And boy did I have one last year; it's still growing out. Nevertheless, I managed to take out my frustrations on the walking path, and when I hit rock bottom, I binged on carrots until my jaw hurt.

EXCUSE ME! EXCUSE YOU!

A reason is a noun, pronounced 'rē-zᵊn. It is a statement offered in explanation or justifica-

WHAT'S YOUR EXCUSE?

Slow Metabolism • Genetically Cursed • Addicted to Almonds • I Buy Cookies for My Kids • I Just Can't • It's So Hard • It's Too Hard • My Husband Is Skinny & Eats a Lot & I Have to Eat with Him • I Don't Want to Insult the Host • I Am Stressed • Tired • My Illness Made Me Eat • The Rain Made Me Eat • I'm Depressed • I'm Bored • I'm Anxious • I'm Sad • I'm Happy • I'll Start on Monday • Start Tomorrow • I Love Food • Food Equals Love • Addicted • Can't Quit • Can't Give Up Chocolate • Food Is My Friend • Simply Not Inspired • Food Calms Me • Guilt • Member of the Clean-Plate Club • Quit Smoking • I'm Hungry • I Can't Exercise • It's the Drugs I'm Taking • I'm Perimenopausal • I'm Postmenopausal • I'm Prepubescent • College Food • My Lifestyle Is Not Conducive • It's Winter • It's Summer • No Time for Exercise • No Time to Food Shop • Not Motivated • I Can't Afford to Eat Healthy • Can't Afford a Trainer • Can't Afford to Join a Program • I Just Can't Afford It • I'm Healthy for a Few Days but . . . • I've Tried Before • I Always Fail • I Eat Out a Lot • It's My Birthday • Lots to Celebrate • Travel Makes It Impossible • I'm Trying • I'm Too Busy to Focus • Not a Good Time • I'm Injured • I Always Fall Off the Wagon • I'm Doomed • I'm Overwhelmed • Too Old • Too Young • I've Been This Way My Whole Life • I Don't Just Fall Off the Wagon; I Lose Track of the Entire Trail Ride. Well, Everything but the Chow Wagon. • Being a Mom (Triplets, No Less) • Honey, in the Spirit of Solidarity You Need: My Mother and I Have a Teenager • Sugar Addiction • Failed So Many Times, Am Afraid to Try Again • It's Too Hot to Go Out and Exercise • It's Too Cold to Go Out and Exercise • My TiVo Isn't Working and I'll Miss My Favorite Show • Just Don't Care Anymore • I'm Sixty and Don't Think It Matters Anymore if I Am 50 Pounds Overweight . . . but Really I Do • I Don't Get Enough Sleep • I Don't Want To • My Mother Didn't Praise Me as a Child • My Mother Was an Overeater • All the Women in My Family Are Fat • Quality Control— I'm a Catering Director of a Hotel, Constantly Around Food, Talking About Food, Trying New Menu Items, etc.—"It's My Job to Taste the Food" • The Devil Made Me Do It! • I'm Big Boned! • Most of the Above! • All of the Above!

tion, something that supports a conclusion or explains a fact.

An excuse is a transitive verb, pronunced ik-'skyüz. It means to make apology for; to try to remove flame from; to serve as excuse for; to justify. (Source: Merriam-Webster's Dictionary)

FAMILY (MOTHERS, FATHERS, SONS, DAUGHTERS, HUSBANDS, DOGS, CATS)—The best excuses ever.

❊ NEW POINT OF VIEW

There are reasons, and then there are excuses. What may be a valid reason for one person may be an excuse for another. I am hip to my excuses. It's time to tell the truth. ❊

FORGIVERCIZE
The "Tell the Truth and Nothing but the Truth Excusercize"

No matter how much progress we are making in our lives, there are certain areas that we'd prefer not to look at in full light. We'd rather sweep certain upsets under the rug. We are masters at avoidance, rationalization, and denial.

Telling yourself the truth, while sometimes painful, is the compassionate thing to do.

Be the observer. For one day from morning till night, stand back and observe your life. Don't stop yourself from living the way that you do, just observe it.

For instance, if you grabbed a bag of corn chips for breakfast and rationalized your choice by noting that it was only 110 calories for the bag, simply note it.

If you said, "It's cloudy outside. I'll wait till the sky clears to power walk around the park," simply note it.

If you called in sick to work for the sixth time in three weeks, note it.

If you had a few unpleasant interactions with friends or colleagues, note it.

You are no longer mindlessly moving through the day. You are affording yourself an opportunity to take a clear look at your life and note where some tweaks and adjustments may be needed. You are looking at your life from an honest vantage point.

Keep a notebook. First write down your observations in their totality. And then the next day, after you've had a rest from being the observer, be your own best coach. Take a look at your list and ask yourself:

- What patterns do I see?

- What did I learn about myself?

- Did I have any lightbulb moments?

- Was there a particular high point in the day? A particular low point?

- How can I act on what needs to be acted upon?

At the very least, be honest with yourself.

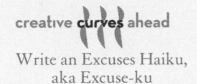

Write an Excuses Haiku, aka Excuse-ku

Utilize the above list of excuses or your own list of excuses!

Haiku, a form of Japanese poetry, consists of a pattern of approximately five, seven, and five phonetic units (i.e., syllables).

Here's my excuse-ku.

No time to food shop
Too busy eating cupcakes
Sugar addiction

Your turn! (If you would like to submit for consideration to be published in Our Lady of Weight Loss's weekly e-letter, Kick in the Tush Club, e-mail it to me!

(Janice@ourladyofweightloss.com)

NO EXCUSES GARLIC CHICKEN

SERVINGS: 4

INGREDIENTS

3 heads of garlic
8 ounces whole-wheat penne pasta
1 teaspoon plus 1 tablespoon extra-virgin olive oil
1 whole skinless chicken breast, diced into half-inch pieces
1 bunch broccoli, cut into medium pieces
½ cup chicken stock
salt and pepper, to taste

INSTRUCTIONS

1. Preheat the oven to 375°F.
2. Cut the tops of the heads of garlic so the top of the clove is exposed. Put them in foil, drizzle them with 1 teaspoon of olive oil, and wrap them into a neat package. Roast them in the oven for 1 hour. Remove them from the oven, let them cool slightly, open the foil, and squeeze out the garlic paste into a small bowl. Set it aside.
3. Cook the pasta according to the package instructions.
4. While the pasta is cooking, heat a large frying pan and add the

Nutrition Facts		
Serving Size (269g)		
Servings Per Container 4		
Amount Per Serving		
Calories 350	Calories from Fat 70	
		% Daily Value*
Total Fat 8g		12%
Saturated Fat 1g		5%
Trans Fat 0g		
Cholesterol 20mg		7%
Sodium 120mg		5%
Total Carbohydrate 54g		18%
Dietary Fiber 9g		36%
Sugars 5g		
Protein 19g		
Vitamin A 20%	•	Vitamin C 230%
Calcium 10%	•	Iron 15%

*Percent Daily Values are based on a 2,000 calorie diet. Your daily values may be higher or lower depending on your calorie needs:

	Calories	2,000	2,500
Total Fat	Less Than	65g	80g
Saturated Fat	Less Than	20g	25g
Cholesterol	Less Than	300mg	300 mg
Sodium	Less Than	2,400mg	2,400mg
Total Carbohydrate		300g	375g
Dietary Fiber		25g	30g

Calories per gram:
Fat 9 • Carbohydrate 4 • Protein 4

remaining tablespoon of olive oil. Add the chicken pieces and cook them until they are browned.

5. Add the broccoli, chicken stock, and roasted garlic paste. Season with salt and pepper and stir to combine

6. When the pasta is al dente, drain it (do not rinse it, and reserve some of the pasta water) and pour the pasta into the chicken mixture. Toss it and cook it for 1 minute. Add more pasta water if needed.

7. Serve immediately.

"E" STOP 34

PUT ON YOUR DANCING SHOES

Further along in my exploration of exercise outside the gym, I found that there is no disputing it: whether you're spinning on the dance floor doing the Latin hustle or circling to the right as the square dance caller sings out the moves, you're getting exercise—and having fun!

Dancing not only burns calories, it offers an opportunity to socialize with friends, make new friends, partner up and hoedown—and much more.

- Calories—Depending on the type of dance, you can burn between 200 and 400 calories per half hour! That's as much as swimming, walking, or riding your bicycle. One of the factors that determines how many calories are burned is the ground you've covered. Researchers have found that square dancers cover five miles in a single evening!

- Cardiovascular conditioning—Dancing can lead to a slower heart rate, lower blood pressure, and an improved cholesterol profile. The degree of cardiovascular conditioning depends on how vigorously you dance, how long you dance, and how regularly you do it. Suffice to say, three to four times a week of thirty to forty minutes of vigorous dancing is considered real exercise.

- Strong Bones—Many dances incorporate side-to-side movements, which strengthen your weight-bearing bones and can help prevent or slow the loss of bone mass, also known as osteoporosis.

- Mayo Clinic researchers report that dancing reduces stress, increases energy, improves strength, and increases muscle tone and co-ordination.

- Dancing is good for the brain. It increases blood flow to the brain and provides mental challenges (as it requires memorizing steps and working with a partner), both of which are central to brain health.

- Sociability—Last, but most definitely not least, dancing contains a social component that many other forms of exercise do not. And sociability, making friends, and developing relationships can give your self-esteem a major boost and give you a positive outlook on life!

So get moving—do the waltz, the fox-trot, or the Latin hustle, or grab your partner's arm and do the do-si-do!

DANCE IT OFF!

Here's an approximation of how many calories you might burn per hour, based on someone who weighs approximately 150 pounds.

- Aerobic dancing: 540+
- Ballet: 300
- Ballroom dancing: 265
- Belly dancing: 380
- Salsa dancing: 420+
- Square dancing: 280
- Swing dancing: 235

Svelte Talk

DANCING—A rather painless way to be active (code word for exercise) while you partner up and "hoe down"—emphasis on "hoe."

CARDIOVASCULAR CONDITIONING—Getting your heart pumpin' love and excitement.

✳ NEW POINT OF VIEW

It's hip to be square while you burn calories to boot! ✳

SIN CITY

The Devil Made Me Do It!

I whispered "no butter,"
hoping that the waiter couldn't hear me.

Oops, you took a wrong turn!

You are lost in Sin City and have committed waiter fraud.
   The food police have arrested you.

Cash in one of your Get Out of Jail Free cards or take elocution lessons, making sure your voice is strong and can be heard, no matter the whisper, and say the following tongue twister ten times fast:

Betty Botter had some butter,
"But," she said, "this butter's bitter.
If I bake this bitter butter,
It would make my batter bitter.
But a bit of better butter,
That would make my batter better."
So she bought a bit of butter—
Better than her bitter butter—
And she baked it in her batter;
And the batter was not bitter.
So 'twas better Betty Botter
Bought a bit of better butter.

Get Out of Jail Free Card

The Sin City food police
have arrested you.

This card may be kept until
needed. It is nontransferable

All is forgiven, move on

VALLEY 35 OF THE CHEERS

MELT THE FAT AWAY

The Our Lady of Weight-Loss Cheerleaders present *a song . . .*
"Melt the Fat" by Myrna M.

(Sing to the tune of "Row, row, row your boat.")

Melt, melt, melt the fat,
Eat less every day.
Melt, melt, melt the fat,
Watch it fade away.

Melt, melt, melt the fat,
Exercise every day
Melt, melt, melt the fat,
Watch it fade away.

Melt, melt, melt the fat,
Pedal it away
Melt, melt, melt the fat.
Watch it fade away.

87

STEP 36

DO *NOT* TRY!

"Do or do not . . . there is no try."
—*Yoda, Star Wars*

The most sabotaging word in the English language—and therefore in the Battle of the Bulge—is the word "try." The implicit possibility of failure is always there. You've left yourself a loophole and somewhere in the back—or the front—of your mind, you may hear a little voice saying, "You might not—you will not—how do you think you are going to—make it."

There are other words and phrases that you can use instead of "try" that have a positive association to them.

Eliminate the word "try" from your vocabulary, and substitute the words—

Explore
Discover
Learn
Search
Investigate
Find out more about

Tune in to yourself. When you hear yourself using the word "try," substitute one of the above words and notice how the meaning and feel of the whole sentence changes.

Svelte Talk

TUNE IN—Stop! Listen and learn. A solo inner activity. There are no dials or remote controls involved.
FAILURE—An opportunity to do again.

FORGIVERCIZE
Behavioral Tweaking Encouraged

What behaviors do you want to modify (adjust, alter, amend, vary, revise)? Changing everything all at once is a bit overwhelming, but revising and adjusting—giving a good tweak here and there—is doable.
    For example:

    _____ One one-ounce piece of candy daily (instead of three candy bars)
    _____ Wake up thirty minutes earlier three days a week (instead of getting up three hours earlier daily, thinking you're going to hit the gym and work up a sweat when you never have before.)
    _____ Carve out fifteen minutes of quiet time four days a week and just breathe (instead of thinking you are going to spend an entire hour meditating daily for the rest of your life).

creative **curves** ahead

Have an Apple Brown Betty contest! Invite all your friends to make their own version of apple brown betty (stipulating that each serving is under 300 calories—in other words, no heavy cream, whipped cream, or lard, if you please). Line up the different apple brown betties with tiny (and I mean tiny, folks) tasting plates and vote. It's a takeoff of the movie *State Fair* (very old—before my time—but nonetheless a favorite). If you catch it you can sing "My state fair is a great state fair . . . " while tasting. Or watch the movie. There are two versions, one from 1945 and one from 1962—both corny as ever, but totally fun, as any Rodgers and Hammerstein musical might be!

APPLE BROWN BETTY

It's an American dessert that dates back to colonial times. A "betty" is a baked pudding made with layers of sweetened and spiced fruit and buttered bread crumbs. It's usually served with some kind of cream. Not here, though. Forgetaboutit!

SERVINGS: 8

INGREDIENTS

6 golden delicious apples, sliced
¾ cup frozen apple juice concentrate
½ cup golden raisins
1 teaspoon ground cinnamon
⅓ cup whole-wheat flour
⅓ cup quick oats
3 tablespoons packed dark brown sugar
3 tablespoons butter

INSTRUCTIONS

1. Preheat the oven to 375°F.
2. Coat a medium-size baking dish with nonstick spray. Set it aside.

Nutrition Facts		
Serving Size (157g)		
Servings Per Container 8		
Amount Per Serving		
Calories 210	Calories from Fat 45	
		% Daily Value*
Total Fat 5g		**8%**
Saturated Fat 3g		**15%**
Trans Fat 0g		
Cholesterol 10mg		**3%**
Sodium 40mg		**2%**
Total Carbohydrate 43g		**14%**
Dietary Fiber 4g		**16%**
Sugars 21g		
Protein 2g		
Vitamin A 4%	•	Vitamin C 45%
Calcium 2%	•	Iron 6%

*Percent Daily Values are based on a 2,000 calorie diet. Your daily values may be higher or lower depending on your calorie needs:

	Calories	2,000	2,500
Total Fat	Less Than	65g	80g
Saturated Fat	Less Than	20g	25g
Cholesterol	Less Than	300mg	300 mg
Sodium	Less Than	2,400mg	2,400mg
Total Carbohydrate		300g	375g
Dietary Fiber		25g	30g

Calories per gram:
Fat 9 • Carbohydrate 4 • Protein 4

3. In a large bowl, combine the apples, apple juice concentrate, raisins, cinnamon, and 3 tablespoons of the flour. Spoon the mixture into the prepared baking dish.
4. In a medium bowl, combine the oats, brown sugar, butter, and remaining flour. Stir the mixture until it is crumbly. Sprinkle it over the apple mixture.
5. Bake the pudding for 1 hour, or until it is bubbly and golden brown. Serve it warm. Yum!

STEP 38

KILL YOUR APPETITE . . . NOW!

Instead of trying to kill your appetite (no need to be so violent) and treating it as though it were your mortal enemy, you might want to consider making appetite your friend—a valuable, intelligent friend to whom you pay attention!

Having an appetite is a good thing; even thin people have appetites, and they pay attention to their appetites, don't they?

In the past, you've paid attention to only half the signal from your appetite—the "I'm hungry, feed me" part. That's the part of the signal that tells you to eat. (Nothing wrong with your hearing on that one!)

When that feeling of hunger first starts to disappear, your appetite says, "I'm satisfied." It's important that you pay attention to that piece of your friend's advice. Did you note that I said when that feeling of hunger *first* starts to disappear? That's right. You want to stop eating long before you feel full. Chances are that

once you hit full, you have grossly overeaten and remorse is right around the corner.

(Personal confession: Before Our Lady of Weight Loss entered my life and introduced me to my friend, Appetite, I would eat until I couldn't breathe. Gross, indeed! And dangerous, too!!)

Now pay attention.

You don't want to feel full; you do want to feel satisfied. Your appetite is your friend. Your appetite tells you when you are hungry and when you are satisfied. Listen to your appetite.

Your eating is no longer driven by emotions. Now that you have met your friend Appetite, you can be in close contact with her as she guides you to 'satisfied.'

Svelte Talk

APPETITE—One of the best friends that I've ever had.

✳ NEW POINT OF VIEW

Your appetite doesn't need to be killed off. There's no place or need for violence in the Land of Permanent Fat Removal! ✳

DINING OUT WITH DIGNITY

HOW does one survive a night out with friends? What do you do when the server places the bread basket squarely in front of you and drizzles olive oil for convenient dipping?

I asked my posse of weight-loss buddies if they had any "dining-out secrets" that they'd like to share. Here are a few tips from some of our kickin' sisters and one or two tricks that I learned from Our Lady of Weight Loss.

OUR LADY OF WEIGHT LOSS'S TWELVE-STEP PROGRAM TO DINING OUT WITH DIGNITY

STEP #1: ORDER OFF THE MENU
The restaurant wants your business, so even if the word broiled, steamed, or poached is not on the menu, you can request that form of cooking. Be assertive, not aggressive. Assertive means asking, even insisting. Aggressive means

storming into the kitchen and hurting the chef. (Let's keep the police out of this.)

Step #2: Get twice as much bang for your calorie buck

Choose fish or skinless chicken over meat. (One ounce of fish and chicken is approximately 50 calories; one ounce of meat is approximately 100 calories). Be sure to say "dry, no butter" at least three times.

Step #3: Order an appetizer as your main course

It's more than likely enough food.

Step #4: Say "super-size me" when ordering salad

(You heard right, the one and only time you can say it—just for salads—so say it loud and be proud.) Request the (low-fat, if available) dressing "on the side." Alternatively, squeeze some fresh lemon, sprinkle some salt and pepper, and you're good to go. Then do "The Fork Trick." Dip the fork in the salad dressing, spear some salad with the fork, then eat. Be careful not to unconsciously dip the salad in the dressing first. Got it?

Step #5: Order up a platter of steamed vegetables and then self-"esteam" yourself

Even if sautéed they will more than likely be swimming in butter or oil. Be sure to say "no butter" at least three times, followed by three nice things about yourself. (I am fabulous and

funny. I was brave to ask for something off the menu. I look terrific.)

Step #6: Potatoes are not the enemy!

Order a baked potato with plain yogurt on the side. Or a sweet potato—truly delicious, plain and simple.

Step #7: Eat low to high

Start with the lowest-calorie foods first, so by the time you get to dessert, you're full.

Step #8: Eat slowly and masticate your food

Chew your food until it's pureed! And put the fork down between bites. You don't want to finish while everyone else is still chewing away. (It could get ugly.)

Step #9: Scream, "I'm allergic"

If you get a sense that they don't get what you are saying, just tell them that you are highly allergic to butter and oil. (I've done this on more than one occasion. It is always fun to watch my husband's eyes roll to the back of his head.)

Step #10: Sip slowly

A glass of wine is approximately 120 calories. One glass is okay.

Step #11: Share

Order one dessert. It's okay to take a bite or even two. Savor it. Unless it's a red-light food and is going to send you over the edge. In that case, order fresh fruit.

STEP #12: ALMOST FORGOT—THE HOLY BREAD BASKET

What to do? Have a piece (or not—your choice), and then, as quickly as you can, move that basket as far away from you as possible.

✳ NEW POINT OF VIEW

I order off the menu—in the restaurant and in life! ✳

Svelte Talk

DIGNITY—Being able to leave the dinner table without evidence of struggle. No crumbs, spilled wine, or tear-stained dresses.

> ### FORGIVERCIZE
> #### The Dining Out Visualization
>
> **B**efore you leave for your fabulous dinner with friends, loved ones, or a special date, just for a few moments, sit quietly, take in a deep breath, and imagine how you might want to feel at the end of the evening.
>
> Do you want to be kickin' yourself in the tush for overeating?
>
> Do you want to feel proud that you were able to taste the dessert without having to eat the entire pie?
>
> Do you want to be smilin', laughin', or cryin'?
>
> Is it okay with you if you want to take the meal off and jump right back on the wagon afterward?
>
> There are no right or wrong answers. It's all about awareness, planning ahead, and consciousness. The one thing you don't want to do is pretend that you're not going to eat it and then eat it all, giving license to brutal beating-up of self. No cruelty allowed!

creative curves ahead

Pit Stop: Spoken Word

Read the menu with feeling and give it a hip-hop beat.

Butter-milk pan-cakes
three stacked
topped
with your choice of
ba-na-nas or straw-berries
served with
maple syr-up.

STEP 40

SINFUL FEELINGS

"Size matters not. . . . Look at me. Judge me by size, do you?"
—*Yoda, Star Wars*

When did all the madness begin? My dear friend Janet, from North Carolina, told me that she can remember wishing on eyelashes (remember that?) when she was maybe four or five years old for a fast metabolism! Imagine, at four years old her deepest desire was for a fast metabolism. (She was an advanced child.) It was then that she started to equate food with sin, guilt, and lunacy.

THE "BAD" FEELINGS STARTED (MORE OR LESS WITH MY GRANDMOTHER)

Have you ever wondered when people started to obsess about food and weight? There was a time when no one "dieted" and nasty fat words didn't exist. Oh yeah—cavemen didn't call each other fat slobs. Those types of words weren't created until the late 1800s!

Cases of dieting were documented over one thousand years ago, such as William the Conqueror (1028–1087), who tried drinking extra wine as a substitute for food after getting so fat that he had trouble staying on his horse. But our obsession with dieting took root at the end of the nineteenth century.

LET THE "BAD" TIMES ROLL!

In fact, the first fat-ass, corpulent words were "porky" in the 1860s, "jumbo" in the 1880s, and "butterball" in the 1890s. By the time World War I rolled around, being fat was deemed unpatriotic!

Food was plentiful, and Americans were wolfing it down with a vengeance. Health reformers declared the endless supply of meats, cakes, and pies immoral. They preached that gluttony was a gateway to sinful sexual practices (woo hoo!). In addition, they proclaimed that gluttony caused constipation and indigestion.

As Americans entered the twentieth century, interest in weight loss grew. "Experts" offered a number of surefire solutions—magic bullets flying everywhere. Somewhere between the main course and dessert, dieting became a national preoccupation. A multibillion-dollar industry was born.

It's not quite clear why dieting took hold (and hasn't let go since), but theories point to the abundance of food, the increase in sedentary jobs, public transportation, and corsets being out of vogue.

Svelte Talk

METABOLISM—A mysterious bodily function steeped in science that we love to blame for our lack of ability to burn fat.

✳ NEW POINT OF VIEW

I do not accept delivery of my ancestors' nasty terminology or fat genes. ✳

SINFULLY DELICIOUS PORTOBELLO MUSHROOMS AND GOAT CHEESE

SERVINGS: 4

INGREDIENTS

4 large portobello mushroom caps
1 cup canned marinara sauce
4 ounces reduced-fat goat cheese, cut into 1-ounce pieces
2 tablespoons finely chopped pitted black olives
1 tablespoon finely chopped parsley
1 tablespoon finely chopped chives

INSTRUCTIONS

1. Preheat the oven to 375°F
2. Clean the portobello mushroom caps with a damp towel, and with the help of a small spoon, scrape out the gills. Set the mushrooms aside.
3. Spread the marinara sauce in the bottom of a 9 x 9" baking dish.
4. Arrange the mushroom caps, gill side up, over the marinara sauce.
5. Place 1 ounce of goat cheese on each mushroom.
6. Sprinkle the olives, parsley, and chives over the mushrooms.
7. Bake the dish uncovered for 30 minutes or until it is hot and bubbly.

Nutrition Facts		
Serving Size (118g)		
Servings Per Container 4		
Amount Per Serving		
Calories 80	Calories from Fat 40	
		% Daily Value*
Total Fat 4.5g		**7%**
Saturated Fat 2g		**10%**
Trans Fat 0g		
Cholesterol 5mg		**2%**
Sodium 410mg		**17%**
Total Carbohydrate 7g		**2%**
Dietary Fiber 1g		**4%**
Sugars 0g		
Protein 4g		
Vitamin A 8%	•	Vitamin C 10%
Calcium 2%	•	Iron 4%

*Percent Daily Values are based on a 2,000 calorie diet. Your daily values may be higher or lower depending on your calorie needs:

	Calories	2,000	2,500
Total Fat	Less Than	65g	80g
Saturated Fat	Less Than	20g	25g
Cholesterol	Less Than	300mg	300 mg
Sodium	Less Than	2,400mg	2,400mg
Total Carbohydrate		300g	375g
Dietary Fiber		25g	30g

Calories per gram:
Fat 9 • Carbohydrate 4 • Protein 4

SIN CITY

♣ ♣ ♣ ♣ ♣ ♣ ♣ ♣ ♣ ♣ ♣ ♣ ♣ ♣ ♣ ♣

The Devil Made Me Do It!

When the holidays were over, and all my guests had gone home, I was hit with a case of the blues. I went to my old friend the refrigerator for solace. She did not disappoint. There it was—a tube of those delicious Pillsbury Orange Rolls that I had bought to serve but managed to forget. Naturally, I decided to bake them up. I ate one right out of the tube. I baked the rest and proceeded to eat four that night. When I woke up the next morning, I couldn't even bend my fingers because they were so bloated and yeasty (I have a yeast sensitivity, which I already knew about). This was the first time I could see an immediate and blatant connection between what I eat and how I feel! It was somewhat of a revelation! And yet I proceeded to eat the last three rolls, just to get it out of my system. . . . —Susan, Big Sky Country

Oops, you took a wrong turn!

You are lost in Sin City and have committed a "blues" offense—overstocking the fridge, eating raw dough, and baking excessively. Not to mention eating said baked goods.

The food police have arrested you. Either cash in one of your Get Out of Jail Free cards or drink an extra four (eight-ounce) glasses of lemon water immediately to flush out the salt, toxins, and memory of sugary rolls. (This is based on the assumption that you are already drinking at least eight glasses of water per day.)

Get Out of Jail Free Card

The Sin City food police have arrested you.

This card may be kept until needed. It is nontransferable

All is forgiven, move on

STEP 42

AFTERNOON DELIGHT

It's three or four o'clock in the afternoon, and you are sinking fast. As your blood sugar starts its downward swing, your body clock slowly shifts into its natural lull. Your motivation, enthusiasm, and energy have come to a screeching halt. (Understandable, no? You are going against your natural lull, your inner clock!)

You are tempted to stick your hand into the ubiquitous bowl of office candy, grab a soda or a cup of coffee, or hit the vending machine for a bag of chips. Candy, cookies, chips, oh my!

Be forewarned! These snacks are "empty calorie" foods that are laden with sugar and fat. At best, you'll get a temporary jolt, setting the downward spiral into overdrive. They are not the solution.

HOW BEST TO WARD OFF THE EVIL AFTERNOON SLUMP?

Choose a snack that is designed to get your blood sugar on track and send you happily into high gear once again, churning out the work and the smiles. Remember, snacks aren't meant to "fill you up," but rather help you to be "not hungry."

PEANUT BUTTER ON A RICE CAKE—Yum! Measure out one tablespoon of peanut butter and carefully and evenly spread it over two rice cakes. If possible, toast the rice cakes. They are

transformed from Styrofoam to an exotic, crunchy treat.

WHOLE-GRAIN CEREAL WITH LOW-FAT MILK— Buy some miniboxes of healthy cereals (not the high-sugar kind) to keep on hand with half a cup of low-fat milk.

BABY CARROTS AND HUMMUS—Measure out two tablespoons of hummus onto a pretty, small plate, artistically arrange some carrots around it, and dip away. Double dip if you like.

WHAT ARE "EMPTY CALORIE FOODS"?

An empty calorie food is a food that contains few or no nutrients, but still has calories.

Once again, folks, it's about being prepared. Be a good Permanent Fat Removal Scout, would ya?

Rocky Road to Sveltesville Travelin' Survival Snack Guide

Air-popped popcorn
Animal crackers (those cute little boxes)
Applesauce (individual-size containers)
Apple slices
Baby carrots
Bottled water
Cereal (individual-size boxes) (unsweetened)
Cherry tomatoes
Dried fruit
Fresh fruit
Graham crackers (low-fat)
Pretzels (dipped in mustard)
Pudding (the kind that does not need to be refrigerated) (low-fat)
Rice cakes
String cheese
Turkey jerky
Veggie sticks

Svelte Talk

AFTERNOON DELIGHT—A cup of decaffeinated tea with a spoonful of sunny disposition.

VENDING MACHINES—Machinery from hell, devised to taunt, tempt, and take your money (as well as your dignity).

❋ NEW POINT OF VIEW

I am ready with my arsenal of healthy snacks for the afternoon plunge! Bring it on! ❋

SIN CITY

ψ ψ ψ ψ ψ ψ ψ ψ ψ ψ ψ ψ ψ ψ ψ ψ

The Devil Made Me Do It!

*I ate the entire container of Cool Whip Free
in one sitting, with my finger.*

Oops, you took a wrong turn!

You are lost in Sin City and have committed a finger infraction. The food police have arrested you.

Cash in one of your Get Out of Jail Free cards or take piano lessons and put your (nonsticky) fingers to use!

Get Out of Jail Free Card

The Sin City food police
have arrested you.

This card may be kept until
needed. It is nontransferable

All is forgiven, move on

STEP 43

THE DOG RUN

Creative Act of Weight Loss

walk your neighbor's dog

I bumped into my friend Leslie McIntosh on the Rocky Road to Sveltesville. She shared the following story with me, and I just had to pass it on! Rock on, Leslie!

SOMETIMES YOU JUST NEED A LITTLE "ATTITUDE" ADJUSTMENT

After a long and frustrating day at work, I came home tired and upset with all the problems at my job. My inclination was to head to the refrigerator and ingest it all—cooked or raw! Just gorge myself into oblivion. As I stood there with the fridge door open, I asked myself, "What are you doing?" I shut that door and picked up the phone. I called my neighbor, a wise elder, who had recently had hip surgery. I had been walking her dog on weekends during her recuperation. I told her that I had had a bad day at work and really needed to get out of the house and asked if I could take the dog for a walk.

I knocked on her door, still preoccupied with job issues and still really wanting to eat my frustrations away. When she answered the door and invited me in, I protested, "No, I just want to get the dog and go for a walk." She insisted that I come in "just for a minute," ushered me into the living room, and motioned for me to have a seat on the couch. She then disappeared behind a closed door, leaving me to mutter under my breath, "Oh, great. . . ."

Then *Saturday Night Fever*'s "Stayin' Alive" started playing, the door opened, and out pranced Rambo, her eight-pound Yorkie, dressed in his black leather jacket and metal-studded collar. I almost fell off the couch laughing so hard. My sweet and wise neighbor said, "You sounded a little stressed on the phone, and I thought you needed to lighten up a little." Rambo and I headed out for our walk, he decked out in all his glory and me humming "Stayin' Alive."

❋ NEW POINT OF VIEW

The road is paved with funny stories, happenings, and other people's dogs. My eyes, ears, and heart are open. ❋

Janice
Taylor

108

FASHION STOP 44

DOGGIE WEAR

They (whoever they are) say that owners often look like their dogs. For those of you who do, why not take it a creative step further and dress in a matching or complementary fashion?

Whether your dog is sporting a red winter wrap, a polo shirt with wide stripes, or a pair of shades, you do the same.

Both Cole Haan and Juicy Couture design lines of fabulously chic doggie wear, but I have to say . . . the Isaac Mizrahi Pets Bridesmaid Dress with Belt by the name of "Fresh Bloom" steals the lineup. A bow-WOW statement if ever there was one!

THE CALL OF THE CHEETO

"When the Cheeto calls out to you, if all else fails, change your name."
—*Our Lady of Weight Loss*

When the Cheeto calls my name, I go into a trance state and think it's really my friend, and I answer! Some of it is just a knee-jerk reaction from years and years of erroneous conditioning. So, I thought what to do to break the habit—would it take at least twenty-one attempts? Should I replace it with another? Now, every time I hear the "call of the Cheeto," I work on a crossword puzzle (usually *TV Guide* or *People* magazine or even *Us Weekly*; certainly not the *New York Times*, which would cause enough self-deprecating stress to make me eat).

Every time you hear the "call of the Cheeto," pick up your crossword puzzle book, call someone, do something else! Keep your hands and mind busy until the voice quiets and moves on! Don't get in a funk over the junk [food]!

"HEY, YOU TALKIN' TO ME?"

Is that bag of Cheetos calling your name again? It's time to stand tall, be strong, and answer back!

What to Do? Prepare and Strategize!

- Remember the "15 Minute Rule." If a craving hits, chances are it will pass within fifteen minutes. So sit it out or (even better) walk it out. More often than not, you will have moved past the craving and not given in to the vending machine call.

- Keep healthy snacks on hand for the midafternoon nosedive.

- Spicy foods can overcome taste buds. Have a spiced-up Virgin Mary! (Yum, I think I want one now! Check out Righteous Recipe below.)

- Clean sweep. Make sure there are no candy bars hidden in your desk at work or night table at home.

- Listen to music. Music activates the same feel-good center of the brain that food does!

- Find a friend. If you're in an emotional twist, seek a friendly ear (not an ear of corn).

- Walk on the sunny side. Twenty minutes of sunlight is good for you! If you can't get out, try sitting by a sunny window. Sunlight helps to control food cravings and helps mood in general.

- Breathe deep. We often munch out on junk because we're stressed.

- Get creative. There are other ways to satisfy and satiate. Make art; write; garden; walk backwards.

Svelte Talk

FRIEND—A person; not junk food!

CRAVING—A passing shout-out from the devil.

✳ NEW POINT OF VIEW

The Cheeto is not really my friend. ✳

All Is Forgiven, Move On

creative **curves** ahead

Word Jumble Game

RMNADIEA

_____

EACLOOHCT

_____

RSTWAERSEC

_____

(Answers on page 255.)

Janice
Taylor

THE VIRGIN MARY &
MICHELADA DEL DAVID

 mighty combo!

Virgin Mary

INGREDIENTS

1 cup V8 spicy tomato juice
Dash hot sauce (I like my Virgin Mary really hot)
Dash salt and pepper
Celery salt
Celery stalk
Lime wedge

INSTRUCTIONS

1. Combine the tomato juice, hot sauce, salt, and pepper in a shaker with ice.
2. Shake it up, baby, twist and shout.
3. Dip the rim of the glass in celery salt!
4. Pour the Virgin Mary into a glass and garnish with a celery rib and a lime wedge!

Michelada del David

During a recent trip to Mexico, my friend David was turned on to the Michelada. Essentially, it's a Bloody Mary that substitutes beer for vodka. He visited me and made Michelada after Michelada. I loved the extra salt around the rim. Oh my—a five-star drink! (At least it's got Clamato juice in it. Drink it in moderation! And remember: No driving!)

INGREDIENTS

1 lime
Sea salt
Clamato juice
Mexican beer (such as Sol or Corona)

INSTRUCTIONS

1. Cut the lime in half. Run one half along the top rim of a highball glass.
2. Pour sea salt onto a flat plate and dip the limed rim into the salt.
3. Squeeze the other half of the lime into a glass. Throw in a handful of ice.
4. Fill the glass with clamato juice and beer in equal amounts.

Salud!

STEP 47

I'M EATING 9 TO 5

Forty-four percent of office refrigerators are cleaned only once a month;
22 percent are cleaned just once or twice a year!
Yet most perishable foods have a shelf life of just three to five days!
—Source: ADA/ConAgra foods

You've created a safe haven at home . . . and good thing, too, because when you get to work you realize that the food pushers are out—en masse.

How will you make it through the day when someone comes to you with a piece of birthday cake, retirement cake, baby shower cake, left-over brownies from the corporate luncheon—and that's in just one afternoon.

It's never-ending, but nonetheless, you made a commitment to yourself. You can't let yourself down. You cannot cave!

WHAT TO DO?

Stock your office with the right stuff, just as you stock your home. If there's a refrigerator/freezer and a microwave, you are set! I always kept a supply of low-cal cakes, baked chips, and 94 percent fat-free popcorn available.

Women who work more than nine hours per day are more likely than men to munch on sugary and fatty snacks.

If there's a birthday party, bring your own preportioned, low-fat, low-cal slice of cake.

OFFICE FOOD LIST

Baked chips
Fresh fruit, and some more fresh fruit
Hard-boiled eggs
Low-fat/low-cal yogurt
94% fat-free microwavable popcorn
Raw vegetables, and plenty of them
Seltzer/water
String cheese
Vegetable juice

EAT LUNCH!

Take at least twenty minutes to a half hour (if not the full hour) to get away from your desk and have lunch. Take a break and breathe. If ordering out is a problem, brown bag it. Be prepared!

EAT BREAKFAST!

If you are hungry, you are much more likely to lose control. Have a happy breakfast each morning. Make it a part of your daily ritual.

JUST SAY "NO!"

If the food pusher is still pushing sheet cake—insisting that you have just one piece for this special occasion—just say NO, with conviction. Truthfully, it doesn't even taste that good anyway!

Svelte Talk LUNCH—A midday meal that should be savored and eaten with consciousness.

❋ NEW POINT OF VIEW

I will stock the office fridge with my stuff! And Our Lady of Weight Loss help the person who messes with my food or me! ❋

creative curves ahead
Office Food Labels

I got so tired of people eating my food (truly annoying, because they weren't even watching their weight; they were eating their food and mine!!!) that I made labels that spelled it out loud 'n' clear. Touch my food, mister, and you are in big trouble. Don't mess with me!

Back off, Bud . . .
this is my grub!

(don't make me have to tell you again)

Property of:

_____

NO BITES,
LICKS, or TASTES

Property of:

_____

One person's poison
is another person's comfort.

Steer clear!

Property of:

_____

S🔱N C🔱TY

🔱 🔱 🔱 🔱 🔱 🔱 🔱 🔱 🔱 🔱 🔱 🔱 🔱 🔱 🔱

The Devil Made Me Do It!

I have no eating style. No stopping mechanism.
I just keep on eating . . . and eating . . . and eating.

Oops, you took a wrong turn!

You are lost in Sin City and are lacking style and grace. The food police have arrested you.

Cash in one of your Get Out of Jail Free cards or stock up on preportioned foods, measuring cups, and a food scale.

Get Out of Jail Free Card

The *Sin City* food police
have arrested you.

This card may be kept until
needed. It is nontransferable

All is forgiven, move on

STEP 48

THE CLUTTERLESS PATH
(HARDLY EVER TRAVELED)

A certain person, who shall remain nameless (but her initials are P.G.), said to me, "Are you going to keep your 'fat' clothes, so that when you gain the weight back you'll have something to wear?"

Whoa! No. I am *not!* This is Permanent Fat Removal. Hello!

Nevertheless, thank you to this unnamed person whose "kind" words sent me straight to my closet to make sure that there were no remnants of my past left there to haunt me.

And guess what! There were a couple of outfits from yesteryear hanging there—taking up valuable space (I do, after all, live in New York City, where closets come at a premium)—that for one reason or another I was holding on to.

I gathered what remnants of fat clothing were there, as well as newspapers, magazines, mail—the usual clutter—and got rid of it all. Wow! What a clearing!

ISN'T IT TIME TO LET GO AND DECLUTTER?

Clutter can be anything that you no longer use, need or like, love or appreciate. I suspect that we all have too many possessions, unhealthy habits, and antiquated beliefs, as well as emotions that drain us. It is energizing, invigorating, and healing to free ourselves of clutter. It's a relief.

You want to lighten up? Get rid of what no longer works, what no longer fits, what there is no longer room for. Clutter affects your energy and well-being. Clutter can weigh you down both physically and emotionally. What is cluttering your home is also cluttering your mind.

Don't hold on to these things and feelings—to the past—out of habit or fear. Have faith that if you clear away the old, the new will take its place. Know that new and better relation-ships, jobs, beliefs, and even clothing are on the way. In order to receive, we must be able to clear space and let go. When we cling to possessions or ideals for dear life, it only serves to paralyze us. Eliminate items that make you feel tired and unmotivated. Let it go.

Svelte Talk   **DECLUTTER**—A clearing for new stuff of value.

❋ NEW POINT OF VIEW

If it's too painful to throw it away, I give it away to charity! Last year, more than 58 million people donated to Goodwill. There are more than 3,300 Goodwill donation locations in North America. ❋

FORGIVERCIZE

Get to work and declutter. Toss it, now!

Top 5 Declutter Rules from Our Lady of Weight Loss

The Day Rule: If you didn't read today's newspaper today, it's old news. Toss it.

The Two-Month Rule: If you haven't read those magazines within two months, and the pile is growing, you're not going to. Toss them.

The One-Year Rule: If you haven't worn it, used it, read it, slept with it in over one year, you're not going to. Toss it.

Be Real: Are you really going to cash in any of those "rebate" offers or use those buy-two-get-one-free coupons? The clutter ain't worth it. Toss it.

Buy One, Toss One Free: If you've bought a new pair of shoes, rid yourself of an old pair. Really, how much closet space do you have? Toss them.

PINEAPPLE ICE

Servings: 10

Ingredients
⅓ cup sugar
⅓ cup water
3 cups fresh pineapple chunks
1 quart pineapple juice, unsweetened
2 tablespoons mint, chopped

Instructions

1. In a saucepan, bring the sugar and water to a boil, stirring until the sugar is dissolved, then cool the syrup. In a blender or food processor, puree the pineapple, syrup, juice, and mint.
2. Transfer the pineapple mixture to a shallow baking pan and freeze it, stirring and crushing lumps with a fork every hour, until the mixture is firm but not frozen hard, about 3 to 4 hours.
3. Ice may be made two days ahead and frozen, covered. Just before serving, scrape it with a fork to lighten its texture. Perfect for a warm summer day!

Nutrition Facts

Serving Size (160g)
Servings Per Container 10

Amount Per Serving

Calories 100	Calories from Fat 0

% Daily Value*

	%
Total Fat 0g	0%
Saturated Fat 0g	0%
Trans Fat 0g	
Cholesterol 0mg	0%
Sodium 0mg	0%
Total Carbohydrate 25g	8%
Dietary Fiber 1g	4%
Sugars 23g	
Protein 1g	

Vitamin A 2%	•	Vitamin C 45%
Calcium 4%	•	Iron 10%

*Percent Daily Values are based on a 2,000 calorie diet. Your daily values may be higher or lower depending on your calorie needs:

		Calories	2,000	2,500
Total Fat	Less Than		65g	80g
Saturated Fat	Less Than		20g	25g
Cholesterol	Less Than		300mg	300 mg
Sodium	Less Than		2,400mg	2,400mg
Total Carbohydrate			300g	375g
Dietary Fiber			25g	30g

Calories per gram:
Fat 9 • Carbohydrate 4 • Protein 4

SIN CITY

The Devil Made Me Do It!

I decluttered—tossed the old newspapers, fat clothes, dirty laundry—anything that I could toss, I did. However, in the back of the closet, I found a stash of snacks. From chips to licorice. All individually packed, mind you. No big bags, only small. So I left them there, and slowly but surely, in the quiet of the dark night, I stole into my closet and ate them, until I was found with black-stained licorice teeth.

Oops, you took a wrong turn!

You are lost in Sin City and have been found guilty of harboring a criminal. The food police have arrested you.

Cash in one of your Get Out of Jail Free cards or volunteer to teach nutrition at your local elementary school.

Get Out of Jail Free Card

The Sin City food police have arrested you.

This card may be kept until needed. It is nontransferable

All is forgiven, move on

STEP 50

COUNTING MY ONIONS

can remember, some years back, when I joined one of those groups where people obsess about food and weight for the fourteen millionth time in life (you know what group I'm speaking of, yes?), and the leader announced that there was a change in the point system. Onions were no longer considered "free." They were now to be counted as one whole point!

The air got sucked out of the room. People panicked. People gasped and moaned. And a woman named Mary Sue yelled out, "It's no wonder I'm not losing weight. I haven't been counting my onions." (Meanwhile, Mary Sue had chocolate stains on her jacket! But we won't go there.)

The level of upset was so intense that I thought a committee might be formed to hit the supermarkets, confiscate the onions, and burn them at the stake.

Similarly, when the FDA recently revisited

food labels and announced that yesterday's medium apple was now considered small and that the calorie count for a medium apple had increased from 80 calories to 150 calories, panic filled the airwaves, my phone rang off the hook, and my e-mail in-box was overflowing with alarm! I did, on the one hand, empathize. Really, if you can't count on an apple to be what you need it, want it, expect it to be, what can you count on? Nevertheless, upset aside, I counseled everyone to get a grip.

Truly, if you aren't losing weight, I seriously doubt it's because you had a super-sized apple—or two or even three—and miscalculated its calorie count. For that matter, I am kind of skeptical that onions are the things that stopped you from reaching Sveltesville. It might be the bag of chips, the slice of pizza, that slab of birthday cake, or the constant grazing, mightn't it?

Svelte Talk

ONIONS—Aromatic vegetables that can be baked until their natural sugars are released and they are caramelized, creating a positively guiltless sugarlike rush.

❊ NEW POINT OF VIEW

A large apple does not a fat person make. (Let's not get nutty!) ❊

FRUITY TOOTIE

The Our Lady of Weight Loss Cheerleaders present Fruity Tootie

Fruity tootie
Lemon lime
Let's get funky
Have some wine

Fruity tootie
Lemon lime
Let's get happy
Pick a grape off the vine

Fruity tootie
Lemon lime
Come on y'all
Let's have a soulful time.

Go Our Lady!

STEP 52

TAKE A WALK ON THE MILD SIDE

"Everything is in walking distance if you have the time."
—*Steven Wright*

Take the
'No Cake' Walk Challenge

Creative Act of Weight Loss

Want to meditate but just can't stand the thought of sitting? Try a walking meditation. Become aware of your body in motion. It is an easy way to meditate—great for beginners! And it enhances physical, mental, and spiritual well-being.

A walking meditation is your basic slow, run-of-the-mill walk, with *awareness*! You can walk in circles or in a line, ten steps forward, fifteen back, or twenty to the side, inside the loop or outside the loop. The only thing you need to do is pay attention as your feet touch the ground.

Stay mindful of each step—the sensation, the rhythm, the sound. If your mind wanders (you can bet it will), gently bring your attention back to your feet and the steady motion of walking. I would tell you to think about nothing else, but in so doing, you'd start to think, so I won't. In other words, only pay attention to the step!

A walking meditation allows you to keep

your eyes open. You can walk in a beautiful outdoor setting, like the beach or the park, or you can practice indoors, around your home. You can walk around the edge of your biggest room. Or in and out of rooms. Plot out a walking route. Be one with the wind, the sun, the sounds of nature, as well as the trains, dogs barking, and people talking.

Wander aimlessly. Be mindful of your breathing. Watch it. In and out. Relax your eyes. This is called "soft" vision, and it enables you to focus on nothing, but to experience all.

The benefits of walking meditation are:

It improves concentration.
It invigorates a tired soul.
During stressful times, it may be even more relaxing than sitting.

❋ NEW POINT OF VIEW

If I can walk and chew gum at the same time, I can walk and meditate at the same time. Cool! ❋

---

creative **curves** ahead

Buy a pedometer and use it! Even a walking meditation creates movements and steps. Log them on your pedometer. Each day, "meditate" a little longer! It's the ultimate mind/body experience!

WALK ON THE MILD SIDE OF PASTA

Servings: 4

Ingredients

8 ounces (2–2½ cups) farfalle pasta
1 teaspoon vegetable or olive oil
4 ounces turkey sausage, cut into small pieces
2 small shallots, minced
10 ounces frozen spinach, thawed and drained
½ teaspoon nutmeg
1 teaspoon oregano
1 teaspoon kosher salt
½ teaspoon ground black pepper
½ cup low-sodium chicken stock
¼ cup Parmesan cheese, plus 1 tablespoon to sprinkle on
   individual dishes

Nutrition Facts

Serving Size (228g)
Servings Per Container 4

Amount Per Serving

Calories 370   Calories from Fat 90

       % Daily Value*

Total Fat 10g	**15%**
Saturated Fat 3.5g	**18%**
Trans Fat 0g	
Cholesterol 30mg	**10%**
Sodium 1040mg	**43%**
Total Carbohydrate 51g	**17%**
Dietary Fiber 3g	**12%**
Sugars 5g	
Protein 22g	

Vitamin A 110% • Vitamin C 30%

Calcium 20% • Iron 25%

*Percent Daily Values are based on a 2,000 calorie diet. Your daily values may be higher or lower depending on your calorie needs:

	Calories	2,000	2,500
Total Fat	Less Than	65g	80g
Saturated Fat	Less Than	20g	25g
Cholesterol	Less Than	300mg	300 mg
Sodium	Less Than	2,400mg	2,400mg
Total Carbohydrate		300g	375g
Dietary Fiber		25g	30g

Calories per gram:
  Fat 9 • Carbohydrate 4 • Protein 4

Instructions

1. Cook the pasta according to the package instructions.
2. While the pasta is cooking, heat a large sauté pan and add the oil. Add the turkey sausage pieces to the pan and cook them until they are nicely browned.
3. Add the shallots, spinach, nutmeg, oregano, salt, and pepper. Stir the mixture to combine the ingredients and cook it for a couple of minutes.
4. Add the chicken stock and Parmesan cheese.
5. By now the pasta will be cooked. Save some of the cooking water. Drain it (don't rinse it under water) and put the pasta into the sauté pan with the turkey sausage-spinach mixture. Toss the mixture well. Add some of the pasta water if needed.
6. Sprinkle the dishes with the additional Parmesan cheese and serve immediately.

STEP 54

COUNTING SHEEP IN THE AFTERNOON

Nap time!

Join me on my mission . . . to bring positive energy to the world, through napping!

A LULL IN THE ACTION—
NAPPING, A "NOVEL" IDEA
(AND YOU'LL SEE WHY!)

The modern world puts enormous value on being as productive as possible, which translates to being busy as many hours of the day as humanly possible. On the surface this may make sense, but in actuality we may find ourselves exhausted!

Exhaustion in itself leads to overeating (since your body is sending signals that you are low on energy and need more fuel to get going). When you are exhausted you are also functioning less efficiently, so add to your list feelings of frustration and being overwhelmed.

Your need for some downtime is a natural part of your day. Napping is an opportunity for our minds and bodies to take a break. Many mammals take naps, and it is an important part of the day in other parts of the world. It has nothing to do with how late you stayed out the night before. It has nothing to do with age.

Even short naps can be very beneficial. Thirty-minute naps promote physical well-being and improve memory and mood, twenty-minute naps sharpen your senses and revitalize you, ten-minute naps can improve your mood!

If possible, take a nap at the same time every day and use an alarm clock (initially, anyway, until it becomes a part of your routine).

Svelte Talk

PRODUCTIVITY—Getting lots done without a total meltdown or burnout (unless you are melting and burning fat). **EXHAUSTION—**A sign that napping is needed.

✳ NEW POINT OF VIEW

Napping is essential to my well-being. It's okay to crawl in a corner for a few minutes and close my eyes. ✳

creatıve **curves** ahead

Speaking of crawling in a corner and getting in a few Zs, you may want to consider incorporating a touch of George Costanza into your being!

Bring a pretty throw blanket to work. Drape it over your chair, so it looks like you're simply "decorating." Then clear out the space under your desk. Crawl underneath, as George Costanza did in *Seinfeld* (Episode 152: "The Nap: George is tired and needs to take a nap while at work; he finds the perfect place, under his desk.").

I'm telling you something: George was ahead of his time!

STEP 55

JANNY TAKES ON THE SABOTEUR: TYPE I

Creative Act of Weight Loss ~
Tell 5 people what's eating you.

1 2
"Tell it like it is!"
3 4 5
"Take a load off."

Back in the day, when I had a big boss to boss me about, this one particular big boss stood before my desk, taunting me with a bag of cookies, knowing full well that I am who I am and cookies are not my thing. What a saboteur! I told him not to flaunt it—get those cookies away from me. Instead, he left the bag on my desk. So I took them into the office kitchen, smashed them into smithereens, and left them there. Half an hour later, big boss inquired, "Where are the cookies?" I smiled and said sweetly, "In the kitchen."

Needless to say, I no longer work there . . . and I've since found a more adaptive way to release my upset and anger.

When angry or upset, I seek out five people to tell my tale of woe, and by the time I've told my story to the fifth person, I'm so tired of hearing myself, I'm over it.

TAKING ON THE SABOTEUR

While traveling the rocky road to Sveltesville, you are sure to encounter a saboteur or two. A saboteur is a person who, intentionally or not, tries to sabotage—derail!—your efforts toward your weight-loss goal.

What to Do? Stay Focused.

Perhaps the saboteur in question is just plain jealous that you're losing weight (and they're not). Maybe the saboteur is coming from a place of fear. As you change, he or she may feel confused or even rejected.

Even if the saboteur acts out of innocence, it can still put a dent in your plan. It's your job to stay strong in the face of a sulking friend who doesn't understand why you can't go out for pizza just this one time, or why you won't have a slice of their birthday cake. You're in charge. You're in control.

While I do get a kick out of my own spunky nature, it is probably better to come up with a couple of levelheaded ideas of what to do when the saboteur in your life surfaces.

Counteract the negative with a huge platter of positivity.

1. Seek hopeful and helpful support. Call a friend, go online and check in on your favorite Internet weight-loss message board, or write to Our Lady of Weight Loss (she loves mail).
2. If a friend or family member suggests that you are losing too much weight (oh, they will, trust me), kindly reassure him or her that you are on a balanced and healthy food plan.
3. If your partner or spouse is concerned that you're going to leave him or her when the new you fully emerges, explain that dietary changes only change the way you eat and look—they do not change the way you feel. Love is love—fat or thin.
4. Enlist the saboteur. Have a heart-to-heart talk and tell him or her that you're really serious about losing weight and you need his or her support.
5. Be patient with those around you. It takes time, but they will eventually settle down, and perhaps even follow your good example. Be prepared to share your delicious, low-cal, low-fat, Our Lady–approved food!
6. When all else fails, use the allergy defense once again! (See page 96.)

7. And if you are truly upset, don't forget "The Our Lady Five." I promise you that by the time you've told five people, you'll be ready to forgive the saboteur and move on!

 NEW POINT OF VIEW

I can talk it out, not act it out or eat my way through it. Awesome! ✳

Svelte Talk

LISTEN—To concentrate and pay attention to what someone is saying without feeling compelled to answer.

FORGIVERCIZE
The Our Lady five-o-size

As we know, being prepared is a big part of Permanent Fat Removal. Therefore, there's no point in waiting for a crisis or upset to take out your address book (both old school—your hard-copy Rolodex or address book; and new school—on your computer) and decide whom you are going to include in this illustrious group of friends (and family?) to whom you will bitch 'n' moan.

Start from *A* and go to *Z*, pulling names of possible ventees (you are the venter). Be sure to consider who is capable of just listening. You do not want anyone to fix anything (and some people can't help but try to fix things). You simply want to feel comfortable enough to let out your true self, your true frustration, your true feelings, without worrying about feeling judged.

Pull as many names as you can. Break them up into your "A," "B," and "C" lists, "A" being those who are the most capable of being there for you in a way that you need them to be. When the time comes, start with your A-list people and use your "B" and "C" lists as backup. Not everyone is sitting by a telephone waiting to hear from you, and you want to make sure that you can tell your story to five people consecutively.

This is a telephone exercise, not an e-mail event. You must actually talk and listen to yourself.

STEP 56

JANNY TAKES ON THE SABOTEUR:
TYPE II

"Peace is every step."
—Thich Nhat Hahn

YOU TALKIN' TO ME?

Every so often, someone says something to me about my newly found thinness that is upsetting and sends me reeling. (Yes, it's been six years since I permanently removed over 50 pounds, but it still feels newly found. Until I have lived more years thin than fat, I shall consider myself newly thin.)

Attacks have been made on my "weigh" of life—some critical of my eating style, some of my tight jeans, some of my arched eyebrows.

When we change in any way, shape, or form, it sometimes upsets other people's apple carts. They are unnerved. It's important to remember that it's not about us; it's about them, and there is no truth to what they are saying.

The attacker is more than likely overcome by a flurry of uncomfortable feelings. If they feel threatened by your new lifestyle, your new svelteness, your beauty, your calm, your fabulous hair—anything—they may lash out. Their emotions are spilling out and over.

WHAT TO DO?

- Stay cool, man, real cool. No point in escalating the negative vibes.
- Remember—it's not about you. You are not responsible for the attacker's issues.
- Do not counterattack. If you feel compelled to say something, simply express how you felt when they said what they said. You do not want to escalate the "war."
- Take in a deep breath.
- Say, "No, thanks. I'm good."
- Smile and walk away.

Svelte Talk **SABOTEUR—**One who helps you build your determination muscle.

✳ NEW POINT OF VIEW

I cannot control other people's actions, but I can control my own. ✳

All Is Forgiven, Move On

creative **curves** ahead

Here's something to keep you busy and change your relationship to food. It's no longer about eating it. It's a word game!

Fill-in-the-Name Game

Sloppy _____

Eggs _____

Hamburger _____

Beef _____

Apple Brown _____

Cuppa' _____

Quiche _____

Peach _____

Oh! _____

(Answers on page 255.)

JANNY STUFFS HER BUTTERNUT SQUASH WITH SCRUMPTIOUS SAUSAGE SUMMARILY

A TONGUE TWISTER!
FROM KITT CLUB MEMBER DJ!

SERVINGS: 4

INGREDIENTS

1 butternut squash
½ cup chicken stock
1 pound turkey sausage
1 slice bread, cut into cubes
1 egg, beaten
½ cup frozen peas
1 teaspoon dried thyme
Salt and pepper to taste

INSTRUCTIONS

1. Preheat the oven to 375°F.
2. Cut the squash in half lengthwise, scoop out the seeds, and put it in a baking dish. Spray the squash with nonstick spray and season it with salt and pepper. Pour the chicken stock into the squash's cavity and bake the squash in the oven until it is soft.

Nutrition Facts		
Serving Size (155g)		
Servings Per Container 4		
Amount Per Serving		
Calories 90	Calories from Fat 30	
		% Daily Value*
Total Fat 3g		5%
Saturated Fat 1g		5%
Trans Fat 0g		
Cholesterol 55mg		18%
Sodium 150mg		6%
Total Carbohydrate 10g		3%
Dietary Fiber 3g		12%
Sugars 4g		
Protein 6g		
Vitamin A 15%	•	Vitamin C 25%
Calcium 4%	•	Iron 8%

*Percent Daily Values are based on a 2,000 calorie diet. Your daily values may be higher or lower depending on your calorie needs:

	Calories	2,000	2,500
Total Fat	Less Than	65g	80g
Saturated Fat	Less Than	20g	25g
Cholesterol	Less Than	300mg	300 mg
Sodium	Less Than	2,400mg	2,400mg
Total Carbohydrate		300g	375g
Dietary Fiber		25g	30g

Calories per gram:
Fat 9 • Carbohydrate 4 • Protein 4

3. Remove the turkey sausage from its casing. Spray a medium skillet with nonstick spray and brown the sausage.
4. Add the bread to the browned meat, along with the egg and peas. Remove the mixture from the heat and mix the thyme. Season it with salt and pepper.
5. Scrape some flesh from the neck of the squash down to fill in the seed pocket so the surface is even.
6. Mound the squash with stuffing and place it under the broiler until it is golden brown.

Janice
Taylor

GET FIT FOR CHARITY

WALK THE ALTRUISTIC PATH

Get exercise, burn calories, make new friends, and do some good all at the same time.

Participating in a benefit race or other charitable event may be an effective way of reaching your Permanent Fat Removal goals.

Once you've signed up to participate in a walk or run for charity, and you've asked your friends, family, and colleagues to sponsor you, you've made a real commitment that can provide a tremendous incentive not just to do the race, but to train for it as well.

And you are so focused on that one event that you easily, effortlessly, and enthusiastically get into an exercise routine that is preparing you for that day. Time tends to fly a lot faster when you are looking forward to an actual event than when you are "trying" to drop a size.

Walking for a charity provides an opportunity for you to be a part of a wonderful community of people who share a concern for others and a goal. Chances are you'll want to return the following year, so you may just keep on training for the "reunion."

Here's a partial list of events that you might want to consider. And hey, some of them even give you a free T-shirt for participating! Woo hoo, free stuff . . . if it's free, it's for me!

- The MS Walk (5K and 10K event) is held in more than seven hundred cities nationwide during the spring. The group also organizes other events, including the MS Bike Tour and the MS Challenge Walk. Call (800) 344-4867 or visit www.nationalmssociety.org.

- The Susan G. Komen Race for the Cure, one of the largest 5K runs/walks in the world, is held in more than one hundred American cities and three foreign countries each year. Visit www.komen.org.

- The Great American Cleanup is organized by Keep America Beautiful. It is the largest "spring" cleanup event in the country, drawing more than two million volunteers in thirty-five states. Volunteers search local roads and highways for litter for as long as they like, sometimes making it even more challenging than many 5K walks. Visit www.kab.org.

- The Walk to Cure Diabetes is held in more than two hundred locations by the Juvenile Diabetes Research Foundation. Depending on the city, the event ranges from a one-mile walk to a half-marathon. Visit www.jdrf.org.

- The Kidney Walk is held all over the country from early spring to late fall and is organized by the National Kidney Foundation. Call (800) 622-9010 or visit www.kidney .org.

Svelte Talk

MULTITASKER—A person who does good, makes friends, and exercises all at the same time.

❋ NEW POINT OF VIEW

—I can simultaneously give of myself and shed of myself. A win-win situation! ❋

creative curves ahead

Walking Gracefully

While you might be interested in walking marathons, building strength and endurance, it may serve you well to examine your style of walking. I've noticed that some people are—well, let's say—simply lacking in a certain kind of grace and style. Surely you don't want to be sporting an ungainly gait, do you?

If you waddle, shuffle, bob, strut, swagger, prance, tramp, parade, or walk like a camel (up and down motion), listen up.

The traditional training method of walking while balancing a book (or any other prop) on your head, does force you to keep your body in alignment. Good posture, after all, is the foundation for a graceful walk.

Keep your rib cage vertical, pelvis straight, knees and feet pointing straight ahead.

It is important that you practice walking with books on your head, à la old-fashioned charm school. A simple ten minutes a day will improve posture.

And now, consider this. There's no way (I think, unless you are an Olympian walker), to eat while balancing a book on your head.

Keep books handy at all times!

STEP 59

DRESSING YOUR TABLE FOR SUCCESS

"I worry that scientists will find that lettuce has been fattening all along."
—*Erma Bombeck*

The future belongs to those who believe in the beauty of their dreams.

~ Eleanor Roosevelt

INSTRUCTIONS:
MAKE TOAST. EAT TOAST. BE HAPPY.

Just as we dress for success, we should set our tables for success. One really does feel better and make wiser food choices when the dinner table supports them. Not only does Our Lady of Weight Loss offer some fabulous table-setting tips, she offers an excuse to go shopping! You've got to love that!

And guess what? That's where the calorie burning comes into play. Push that cart up and down those aisles—the more you add to it, the heavier the cart and the more you burn. Burn, baby, burn!

PUT SOME THOUGHT INTO SETTING YOUR TABLE. Studies show that people will eat whatever is put in front of them and that they are actually left feeling more satisfied when using salad-size plates instead of dinner plates.

USE DARK PLATES, as they diminish appetite. (For more on the color blue, see page 199.)

CHOOSE A DARK BLUE OR BLACK TABLECLOTH OR PLACEMATS, in keeping with the "keep me in the dark" theme. (Note: You will not find dark blue dishes or tablecloths in restaurants.)

USE TALL, SKINNY DRINKING GLASSES (as opposed to short, wide ones). Researchers at the University of Illinois found that we will pour less into tall, skinny glasses than short and wide glasses, even though they hold the same amount of liquid.

FILL TWO VASES WITH FRESH FLOWERS. The first is for your dining room table—to create a beautiful and relaxing experience. Choose flowers that delight and feed your soul. The second one should be filled with fresh red flowers and placed at the entrance to your home. The red flowers will infuse you with energy upon entering and inspire you to cook up something fabulous on your clean stove.

PUT CANDLES ON THE TABLE. Watch the flames flicker. Hypnotize yourself. ("I will enjoy one small plate of food.")

NEW POINT OF VIEW

Permanent Fat Removal isn't just about the food and exercise; it's about shopping—for clothing, accessories, and tableware! (Wow! This is way more fun and energizing than I'd imagined!) ✳

STEP 50

CREATE A SOFT, SAFE, AND SNUG ZONE

give yourself a kick in the tush

Pet

Your
Puppy

Imagine yourself walking through your front door at the end of a long day and entering a place where emotional eating, red-light foods (trigger foods), red-light situations (trigger situations)—the "diet torture"—just don't exist. A safe haven where you can sit back, take in a deep breath, and simply relax. A place where your mind is free of "diet clutter," negative messages, and berating and depricating comments.

Think of how happy you'll feel when you create a divinely inspired place where you can and will easily strengthen your resolve and reinforce new behaviors—a place where you can tap into your "thinner core." A place where the color alone fills, sates, and comforts you.

Whether you devote an entire room or simply a corner of a larger area as your zone of safety and comfort is up to you. It need only be a place where you feel out of food's way and away from stress—a place where you can immediately sink into a relaxed state and decompress. That's right. Just let go of the day's stress. Shift your thoughts away from "life" and connect, if only for a few minutes, to yourself.

Your space could be in your basement, attic, garage, or even bathroom, as long as it's far from the maddening crowd. Or you certainly could go the more conventional route and create a sacred space in a corner of your living room, your bedroom, or even your garden.

You want to incorporate objects that put you in a relaxed state of mind:

> Beautiful objects that bring forth an immediate sigh
> Music that soothes your soul
> Flowers that take your breath away
> Art that inspires (Resist family photos. This is *your* space.)
> Books that motivate
> Incense or an aromatherapy diffuser
> Soft blankets with positive messages from www.AFFIRMAGY.com

Svelte Talk

MADDENING CROWD—Those people who take you away from feeling "centered," who jangle, disrupt, interrupt, discombobulate, or cause you to disassociate.

❋ NEW POINT OF VIEW

How exciting! I have created a buffer zone between the world and me. It's easy to peacefully shift from the outside world when the inside world is so cozy, isn't it? Feel lighter! ❋

creative curves ahead

Stroke Something Soft and Just Relax . . .

As you consider the benefits of stroking a soft object, you might like to cozy up next to your cat or dog, take in a deep breath, and say "ahhhhhhhhhhhhhh."

No dog or cat available? A soft, fluffy pillow or satin blanket will do.

BAKED GINGER APPLES

SERVINGS: 6

INGREDIENTS

    6 large apples
    8 ounces ginger ale (or diet ginger ale)
    2 tablespoons brown sugar
    ¼ cup walnuts, chopped
    1 tablespoon fresh ginger, minced

INSTRUCTIONS

1. Preheat oven to 375°F.
2. Peel, halve, and core the apples. Put the apples, cut side down, in a baking dish.
3. Pour the ginger ale over the apples
4. Combine the sugar, walnuts, and ginger. Sprinkle the mixture over the apples.
5. Bake for 20–25 minutes or until the apples are tender.

Nutrition Facts

Serving Size (188g)
Servings Per Container 6

Amount Per Serving

Calories 130   Calories from Fat 30

	% Daily Value*
Total Fat 3.5g	**5%**
Saturated Fat 0g	**0%**
Trans Fat 0g	
Cholesterol 0mg	**0%**
Sodium 5mg	**0%**
Total Carbohydrate 27g	**9%**
Dietary Fiber 4g	**16%**
Sugars 21g	
Protein 1g	

Vitamin A 2%	•	Vitamin C 10%
Calcium 2%	•	Iron 2%

*Percent Daily Values are based on a 2,000 calorie diet. Your daily values may be higher or lower depending on your calorie needs:

		Calories	2,000	2,500
Total Fat	Less Than		65g	80g
Saturated Fat	Less Than		20g	25g
Cholesterol	Less Than		300mg	300 mg
Sodium	Less Than		2,400mg	2,400mg
Total Carbohydrate			300g	375g
Dietary Fiber			25g	30g

Calories per gram:
  Fat 9 • Carbohydrate 4 • Protein 4

STEP 62

RIDE THE FREEDOM TRAIN

"Life is a car wash, and I'm riding a bicycle."
—*author unknown*

THIS IS YOUR LIBERATION DAY

Have you ever imagined waking up one fine day, happily and mysteriously a naturally thin person? I always wanted to wake up thin so I could eat whatever I wanted. I hadn't thought about it in terms of being free from wanting the food.

Portion control? Toss that baby out the window, please! (Like that fabulous movie with Meryl Streep and Albert Brooks, *Defending Your Life*. Yes, heaven is an ever-flowing banquet of pasta made of white flour, freshly grated cheese, and plenty o' sauce, garlic bread—no bad breath—wine, and chocolate desserts of all kinds.) Who wants to count and measure? Pretty much no one.

There would be no consequences: no excess rolls of fat, no high cholesterol, no clogged arteries, no risk of diabetes, no back pain, no bad

imagine being free of food thoughts ...

149

skin or lackluster hair. Just plain bliss from basic gluttony. Bring on those platters!

However, after permanently removing 55 pounds, I learned that freedom was about something else.

WHAT IS FREEDOM?

Freedom is about our capacity to act consciously, in a well-balanced manner. It is about self-determination and inner peace.

And oddly enough, it's about planning our meals, planning our time, and yes, even counting and measuring our food and portion control. Here's the thing. If you take care of all those things, it frees you up—it alleviates guilt and beating up of self. You are now free to move forward with the rest of your life. You only have a certain amount of energy to expend in one day. Why not take care of the things that you need to take care of that fuel your body and spirit, and then spend the rest of the time creating and manifesting what your soul wants?

Svelte Talk

LIBERATION DAY—The day you take responsibility for your life and your fat. After all, 'tis no one else but you who is actually putting the food in your mouth.

✳ NEW POINT OF VIEW

Ultimately, freedom (and free will) is about taking responsibility for my life. Unlimited amounts of sugar-coated, fat-laden foods—whether I were to wake up naturally thin or not—are out. ✳

FORGIVERCIZE
Melt into the Landscape

One day not too long ago, I entered Central Park just when the sunlight was shining softly through the trees and shimmering on the lake. The geese were in formation, flying low, saying hello. And the monarch butterflies were out in force—dozens sucking all the nectar out of the honeysuckle bushes.

I felt very much as if I had stepped into a painting and left behind, outside the gates to Central Park, anything that was weighing me down. The stress, thoughts, and concerns of the day—gone.

From that day forward, whenever visiting the park, I pretend that I am entering a painted landscape that comes to life. A magical place where I can be anyone I'd like to be.

I invite you to either locate a park, a gazebo, or a friend's backyard or find a beautiful photo or painting of a landscape, either physically or metaphorically enter, and take a mental vacation from life for as long as you can manage. Ten minutes, a few hours, the entire day . . . melt into the landscape.

SIN CITY

ψ ψ ψ ψ ψ ψ ψ ψ ψ ψ ψ ψ ψ ψ ψ ψ ψ

The Devil Made Me Do It!

Is it acceptable to eat tacos on the treadmill?
Pizza during Pilates?
Gyros at yoga?
I am guilty as charged.

Oops, you took a wrong turn!

You are lost in Sin City and the food police have arrested you. You are guilty of eating while exercising.

Cash in one of your Get Out of Jail Free cards or get back on the treadmill for one hour daily for one week solid, with no food (or food thoughts) in sight!

Get Out of Jail Free Card

The Sin City food police have arrested you.

This card may be kept until needed. It is nontransferable

All is forgiven, move on

A GOLFER'S DIET

A golfer's diet: live on greens as much as possible.
—*Anonymous*

turnip

First, Let's Walk the Course!

Walking the course (an easy way to log close to four miles!) three to five times a week and carrying your clubs is more beneficial than your golf swing!

A brisk walk can improve both your cardiovascular and lung capacity and your blood flow. Your heart pumps away between 90 and 120 beat per minute. It's gentle fat burning at its best—a low-intensity workout.

Swing That Club!

Swinging your club and bending down to place your ball on the tee or pick it up keeps your joints pliant.

Dig It . . . You're out of the Kitchen and into the Air!

Your body kicks in and produces vitamin D when you're out in the sun. And your brain chemicals act differently, in a good way.

Handicap Me!

Golf is a great leveler. Its handicapping system enables beginners to compete with skilled players. A handicap of 0 is called a "scratch" handicap, and a handicap of 20 is called a "bogey." The handicap measures how well you'd stand up against a "scratch" golfer.

Our Lady of Weight Loss is well aware that some of us have bigger challenges to overcome than others, so she had me design a formula for computing our weight-loss handicaps, enabling us to compete with those with high metabolisms, those who forget to eat, and the gym bunnies of the world.

HOW TO CALCULATE AND USE YOUR WEIGHT-LOSS HANDICAP

NOTE: HANDICAPS ARE EARNED. They are for professional "dieters" only. In order to receive a handicap, you have to have been on at least five diets in your lifetime. (I suspect that qualifies most of us.) This means five different diet plans that you followed for at least five weeks.

INSTRUCTIONS

Step 1: Total the pounds lost in your last diet over the course of the last five weeks you were on said diet.

Step 2: Multiply that number by the number of children you have living at home.

Step 3: If you are living with an adult who insists on eating in front of you and who is insensitive to your weight-loss mood swings, add 1 point. If he or she is truly impossible, add another 3 points.

Step 4: Multiply that number by 3.

Step 5: Divide that number by 5. (Slice off fractions, as you would slivers of cake.)

Step 6: For every 10 points, give yourself one handicap point. Those who have a handicap of 10 or more are called "turnips." (Thus, the above art, in case you were confused.)

HOW TO USE YOUR HANDICAP

The next time someone asks you how much you lost this week, feel free to add your handicap into the equation. This system should level the field for those who are competing at group meetings, in offices, or at home! Or for those who are letting the scales of injustice get to them.

Svelte Talk

HANDICAP—Making lemonade out of lemons. In other works, taking a disadvantage and looking at it from a new point of view, thus turning it into an advantage.

✳ NEW POINT OF VIEW

I can swing with the best of them. Fore! ✳

PEACHY KEEN VINTAGE COBBLER

Be sure to wear vintage golf clothes when eating this dish.

SERVINGS: 2

INGREDIENTS

1½ cups peach slices
2 tablespoons peach nectar
1 teaspoon brown sugar
1 teaspoon mint, finely chopped
1 Social Tea cookie, crumbled

INSTRUCTIONS

1. Preheat the oven to 375°F.
2. In a small bowl, combine the peach slices, peach nectar, sugar, and mint. Toss to combine.
3. Pour the peach mixture into a small baking dish. Top it with the crumbled cookie.
4. Bake the cobbler for 20 minutes or until bubbly.

Nutrition Facts		
Serving Size (167g)		
Servings Per Container 2		
Amount Per Serving		
Calories 100		Calories from Fat 5
		% Daily Value*
Total Fat 0g		0%
Saturated Fat 0g		0%
Trans Fat 0g		
Cholesterol 0mg		0%
Sodium 15mg		1%
Total Carbohydrate 24g		8%
Dietary Fiber 2g		8%
Sugars 12g		
Protein 1g		
Vitamin A 10%	•	Vitamin C 15%
Calcium 2%	•	Iron 10%

*Percent Daily Values are based on a 2,000 calorie diet. Your daily values may be higher or lower depending on your calorie needs:

	Calories	2,000	2,500
Total Fat	Less Than	65g	80g
Saturated Fat	Less Than	20g	25g
Cholesterol	Less Than	300mg	300 mg
Sodium	Less Than	2,400mg	2,400mg
Total Carbohydrate		300g	375g
Dietary Fiber		25g	30g

Calories per gram:
Fat 9 • Carbohydrate 4 • Protein 4

STEP 65

WHAT'S YOUR
ECUMENICAL EATING STYLE?

Green Pepper

In Japan, the most popular Domino's pizza topping is squid.

WHAT'S YOUR ECUMENICAL EATING STYLE?

It has taken us decades to refine and polish our eating styles and systems. I am a master "if it's free, it's for me" eater! Supermarket samples are my downfall; and furniture showrooms with Sunday sales that offer coffee and dough-nuts are simply off limits! There's just so much I can take!

What do our "styles" and "systems" say about us? Perhaps it's time to take a look at our methodology and make some minor (or major) adjustments!

OUR LADY OF WEIGHT LOSS'S TOP TEN ECUMENICAL EATING STYLES

1. THE UNCONSCIOUS EATER
If you find yourself covered in cookie crumbs and do not have any memory of eating cookies, you are an unconscious eater. Wake up! Be in the here and now.

2. GULP N' GO
Are you always on the run, doing the ol' gulp 'n' go? Sit down and take a moment. Please.

3. FOOD ARCHITECT
You are a food architect if you sculpt mountains of mashed potatoes, arrange broccoli in and around them like trees, and layer slices of meat until you've created a high-rise apartment building. While I admire your creativity, play with Legos instead!

4. ASSEMBLY-LINE EATER
You are an assembly-line eater if you load up another forkful while still chewing. Put the fork down in between bites.

5. NEVER SAY, "NO, THANK YOU"
Do you have a "never say, no, thank you" policy in place? Afraid you might offend someone? Time for a rewrite.

6. IF IT'S FREE, IT'S FOR ME
Do you exclaim, "If it's free, it's for me!" when you see free food tastings and samplings at the supermarket? Eat before food shopping and recommit to your goals before you head out.

7. CLOSET EATER
You are a closet eater if you keep a minifridge in your coat closet and visit it nightly. Come on out of the closet and join the rest of us. It's safe out here.

8. SPEED EATER
If your friends suggest that you challenge the Japanese world speed-eating champion, who swallowed a total of 53½ hot dogs, and their accompanying buns, in just twelve minutes, then you are a speed eater. I'm gagging just thinking about it.

9. BEIGE EATER
If potatoes, pasta, and mac and cheese are your mainstays, then you are a beige eater. Add red peppers, strawberries, green beans, and bright blueberries to your palette . . . *now.*

10. FRIED
You are fried if you think "fried" is a food group. Now you know better!

Svelte Talk

CHAMPION—Someone who gets back on the wagon after swallowing 53½ hot dogs in 12 minutes!

❋ NEW POINT OF VIEW
Whatever my style, I'm excited that I've got one! ❋

THE WORLD IS YOUR OYSTER:
EXPECT THE BEST

Gravity always gets me down
—*Anonymous*

YOU GET WHAT YOU EXPECT

It is called the Pygmalion effect, and it's a fact: If you expect the worst, you get it. Thoughts are not just some insubstantial bits of information that enter our minds and fade away into the ether; thoughts are things. Our words, ideas, beliefs—our thoughts—shape our lives.

Thoughts have a profound effect on our capacity to see opportunity and take action. Positive thoughts lay the groundwork and enable us to actualize what we desire.

We create our reality. We are the stars of our dramas. Circumstances do not determine your happiness or unhappiness. You do! When your thoughts are in alignment with your desires, your desires will magically materialize.

And while you may feel absolutely justified as you scream, cry, and carry on over gaining a couple of pounds, you might want to consider whether your actions are ultimately constructive. Does getting upset and angry help? (No. In case you're confused.) It may well catapult you into a downward spiral.

Practicing positivity does not mean that you are a happy idiot. It means that you seek solutions! It means that you understand that you are the pivotal character, the star (not the victim) in your drama. You are responsible. No pity parties!

For instance, let's just say hypothetically that you go to a party in a foreign country where you know no one except the host, and the host is clearly lacking in social graces and does not introduce you to a soul. Do you sit in a chair and smile like a happy idiot? Or, even worse, smile and stuff yourself with chips, dips, and pigs in blankets? No! You are the star of your story. You introduce yourself to the other players, and you have the best time, harboring no ill feelings for the host.

When you cease playing the victim and you feel that you are worthy and that your dreams are within your reach, you are more likely to imagine positive situations with happy outcomes. You easily and effectively navigate the roadblocks.

Happiness is a practice, something to be developed. Exercise your joy muscle.

Svelte Talk

VICTIM—A person in someone else's drama. Certainly not you.

✳ NEW POINT OF VIEW

When defeating thoughts surface, I send them on their way. "Come again, when you can't stay so long," is what I say. ✳

THE WORLD IS YOUR OYSTER
AND IT COMES WITH A SIDE
OF DILL VINAIGRETTE

SERVINGS: 2

INGREDIENTS

2 teaspoons rice wine vinegar
1 teaspoon hot mustard
2 teaspoons chopped dill
½ teaspoon salt
¼ teaspoon ground black pepper
2½ teaspoons olive oil
2½ teaspoons canola oil
12 oysters
1 tablespoon salmon roe (optional)

INSTRUCTIONS

1. Make the vinaigrette: In a small bowl whisk together the rice wine vinegar, mustard, dill, salt, and pepper. In a thin stream, add the oils. Set aside the mixture until you are ready to use.

Nutrition Facts		
Serving Size (63g)		
Servings Per Container 2		
Amount Per Serving		
Calories 150	Calories from Fat 120	
		% Daily Value*
Total Fat 13g		20%
Saturated Fat 1.5g		8%
Trans Fat 0g		
Cholesterol 40mg		13%
Sodium 770mg		32%
Total Carbohydrate 4g		1%
Dietary Fiber 0g		0%
Sugars 0g		
Protein 5g		
Vitamin A 0%	•	Vitamin C 4%
Calcium 4%	•	Iron 25%

*Percent Daily Values are based on a 2,000 calorie diet. Your daily values may be higher or lower depending on your calorie needs:

	Calories	2,000	2,500
Total Fat	Less Than	65g	80g
Saturated Fat	Less Than	20g	25g
Cholesterol	Less Than	300mg	300 mg
Sodium	Less Than	2,400mg	2,400mg
Total Carbohydrate		300g	375g
Dietary Fiber		25g	30g

Calories per gram:
Fat 9 • Carbohydrate 4 • Protein 4

2. Carefully open the oysters, remove them from the shells, and put them in small bowl. Clean the shells and return the oysters to the shells. Put crushed ice on a plate, and put the oysters on top of the ice.
3. Top each oyster with ½ teaspoon of the vinaigrette and then ¼ teaspoon of salmon roe (if desired).
4. Serve immediately.

creative curves ahead

Contact Our Lady of Weight Loss through prayer!

Make up your own prayer, as did Neely McC.! She spent hours working on her prayer (and not eating), and she has made it a part of her morning ritual. Wake up, go to bathroom, brush teeth, make coffee, say prayer while it is brewing.

My Gracious Lady, to you I pray
From the cupcake help my hand to stay

Gluttony would be my deadly sin
Once again I failed to overcome, I admit with chagrin

The siren song of the pink icing
I could not resist, as too enticing

Let veggies and fruit hold such appeal
That my tummy I will once again reveal

Let me remember with the brief pleasure
Comes bloat, sloth, and flatulence without measure

Thank You, Lady, for giving me power
Over my food choices hour by hour

Until once again, to you I pray
It becomes my healthy living day to day.

STEP 68

TRAVELIN' "LITE"

"How come when you mix water and flour together you get glue, and then you add eggs and sugar and you get cake? Where does the glue go?"
—*Rita Rudner*

"Gee, Rita . . . maybe that's why cake stays glued to my thighs."
—*Marsha Coleman*

I well know the mixed bag of emotions that come with traveling. You want to get away, have fun, get some sun, tour the museums in Europe, visit family in Greece, but you are terrified that you are going to lose control and go crackers, or maybe even bananas, aren't you?

Yes, as wonderful as vacations are, they are plenty stressful. So, please allow me to lay my travelin' wisdom upon you!

Ask yourself this: "Do I want to lose weight while I am away, am I happy to stay the same, or might it be okay to gain a pound or two?"

There's no right answer, but it's good to be clear from the get-go. You don't want to say that you're planning on losing weight and then come back a pound heavier and feel like you've failed. So be realistic, and at the same time, remain in control.

HOW TO KEEP YOUR TRAVELIN' LEGS ON THE GROUND!

Your daily routine is disrupted, you're in a different environment, perhaps there's a time zone change, and you may even be in a place where you don't speak the language.

RESEARCH WHERE YOU ARE GOING
Many major hotels provide a minifridge for the asking! Go to the local market and stock it with fruits, veggies, and low-fat snacks. If you don't have time to shop, call and see if they deliver!

MAKE EVERY EFFORT TO EAT THREE MEALS A DAY
No matter where you are, you'll want to keep your energy going. Surely you don't want to get to the point where you're starving, cranky, and ultimately out of control. (Nobody likes a crank.)

PACK SNACKS
My travel kit includes melba toast, healthy energy bars (read the labels; lots are very misleading), one-ounce boxes of raisins, and a small bag of raw cashews. Pretzels and rice cakes are an option as well.

STAY HYDRATED
Carry bottled water with you at all times. And drink it!

WHEN IN RESTAURANTS, refer to "Dining Out with Dignity" (page 95).

STAY FOCUSED!
If you hear yourself saying "It's a vacation," or "One day off is okay," refer back to "Excuses, Excuses" (page 77) and write yourself an excuse-ku.

AS FOR DESSERT!
I always save the big guns for the end of my vacation. If I were to start out saying, "Oh, I'll have dessert just this one night," and it was the first night, I know I'd be in trouble. But the last night—well, then I'm really on vacation!

KEEP OUR LADY OF WEIGHT LOSS WITH YOU at all times (in your thoughts and in your pocketbook). Just in case you need to confess.

Svelte Talk WISDOM—Knowing that when you are on vacation, you may stray. And that's okay.

❋ NEW POINT OF VIEW
I can let a pound or two visit, but not move back in! ❋

Janice
Taylor

164

STEP 69

WHAT A DAY FOR A DAYDREAM!

While waiting for the 6 train on 116th Street and Lexington Avenue (not the most beautiful subway stop in Manhattan), I took the opportunity to mentally review my "to do" list: pick up low-fat milk, watermelon, bags of salad, one-calorie-per-spray dressing; drop off my dry cleaning; call my cousin; sign up for meringue lessons . . .

The thought of learning how to dance the meringue—gliding gracefully and sensually across the dance floor—set my mind off and, well, dancing . . . into a beautiful daydream. I mentally drifted onto the dance floor. I could hear the music, and I could feel my hips swaying. I was energized, happy, and feeling alive.

Just as Antonio Banderas was reaching his hand out to mine, our fingers just about to touch, the train screeched into the station. I didn't get to dance with Antonio, but I realized that daydreaming is a type of trance state.

Daydreaming is a fantasy that one has while

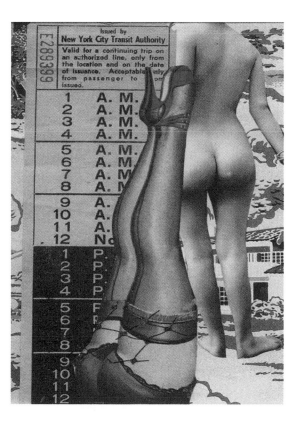

awake—often spontaneous, as was my daydream. Some daydreams are about future scenarios, some replay past experiences, and many are connected to some type of emotional experience.

Einstein daydreamed his way to the theory of relativity. Proof positive that daydreaming stimulates the mind, relaxes the body, and can help to set goals, manage conflict, boost productivity, increase creativity, achieve goals, and relieve boredom. (Go, Einstein, go!)

Svelte Talk

DAYDREAM—Pleasant thoughts and images that pass through the mind while awake, that have the ability to influence your life and help you to manifest what matters to you! A useful way to spend your time. (Better than watching TV.)

 NEW POINT OF VIEW

Daydreaming is as important to Permanent Fat Removal as food and movement (aka exercise). Make it a part of your day. ✳

THE
YOU-DON'T-HAVE-TO-BE-EINSTEIN
TUNA CASSEROLE

SERVINGS: 6

INGREDIENTS

8 ounces wide egg noodles
2 cans tuna in spring water, drained
½ cup low-fat yogurt
½ cup sliced black olives
¼ cup green olives
½ teaspoon salt
¼ teaspon pepper
⅛ cup butter
1 cup breadcrumbs
¼ cup Parmesan cheese
Paprika
Additional black olives for garnish (optional)

INSTRUCTIONS

1. Preheat the oven to 350°F.
2. Boil and drain the noodles.

Nutrition Facts		
Serving Size (207g)		
Servings Per Container 6		
Amount Per Serving		
Calories 420	Calories from Fat 90	
		% Daily Value*
Total Fat 11g		**17%**
Saturated Fat 4g		**20%**
Trans Fat 0g		
Cholesterol 80mg		**27%**
Sodium 960mg		**40%**
Total Carbohydrate 42g		**14%**
Dietary Fiber 2g		**8%**
Sugars 2g		
Protein 38g		
Vitamin A 6%	•	Vitamin C 0%
Calcium 15%	•	Iron 25%

*Percent Daily Values are based on a 2,000 calorie diet. Your daily values may be higher or lower depending on your calorie needs:

	Calories	2,000	2,500
Total Fat	Less Than	65g	80g
Saturated Fat	Less Than	20g	25g
Cholesterol	Less Than	300mg	300 mg
Sodium	Less Than	2,400mg	2,400mg
Total Carbohydrate		300g	375g
Dietary Fiber		25g	30g

Calories per gram:
Fat 9 • Carbohydrate 4 • Protein 4

3. In a bowl, mix together the noodles, tuna, yogurt, sliced black olives, green olives, salt, and pepper.
4. Put the mixture in a two-quart casserole dish.
5. In a small bowl, melt the butter. Add the bread crumbs and cheese.
6. Pour the breadcrumb mixture over the noodle mixture.
7. Sprinkle paprika on top.
8. Bake the casserole uncovered for 35 minutes.
9. Optional: "Write"out "Happy Birthday, Albert" with black olives on the top of the casserole.

Janice
Taylor

BACK IN THE SADDLE AGAIN

"How did the eggs leave the highway? Through the 'eggs-its.'"
—*author unknown*

If you've fallen off the wagon as many times as I, and you're yellin' out, "Help!!! I've fallen off the wagon and I can't get up!!!" you've come to the right place.

THE EGG STORY—FOOD FOR THOUGHT!

You've decided to make scrambled eggs for breakfast. You take three eggs from the refrigerator. As you are oh-so-gracefully moving toward the counter, one falls from your hand and smashes on the floor.

What do you do?

1. Clean it up.
2. Make two scrambled eggs instead of three.
3. Get another egg from the fridge.
4. Throw the other two eggs on the floor and say "screw it."

The Egg Story

169

Weight loss is a process. Falling off the wagon and finding yourself a bit bruised and bloated is par for the course. There's no need to throw your eggs on the floor and give up!

Those who reach their weight-loss goals are simply the ones who get back on the wagon—again and again. (Personally, I've fallen so many times, it's become a part of my exercise program.) Those who succeed experience these setbacks as temporary lapses. They understand that there are no magic bullets, no quick fixes. The turtle wins this race.

Here are a few thoughts and tips to help you pick yourself up and climb back on the wagon!

HOW TO PULL YOURSELF UP BY THE BOOTSTRAPS IN FIVE EASY STEPS

1. *Practice Loving Kindness.* Please stop being hard on yourself and saying mean things to yourself! (If someone else called you a fat pig, you'd punch them in the nose!)
2. *Postcards from the Edge.* Send inspirational and motivational weight loss e-cards to your friends. Helping others stay on track helps you keep yourself on track. Here's a link to the best e-cards ever—and they're free: http://www.ourladyofweightloss.com/e-cards/.
3. *Write Out Your List of Reasons.* I want to lose weight because I want to _____. (Fill in the blank, and be honest.) "Be healthy. Look younger. Be socially acceptable. Make that rat who left me feel real bad."
4. *The 80/20 Rule.* No one is perfect 100 percent of the time. If you follow your weight-loss plan 80 percent of the time and treat yourself

to an occasional treat 20 percent of the time, you should be able to achieve and maintain your weight-loss goals.

5. *Five Easy Pieces.* Listen to the five "easy" classical pieces played in the movie *Five Easy Pieces* (1970).

- Chopin's Fantasy in F Minor, op. 49, played by Dupea on the back of a moving truck.
- Bach's Chromatic Fantasy and Fugue, played by Dupea's sister, Partita, in a recording studio.
- Mozart's Concerto in E-flat Major, K. 271, played by Dupea's brother, Carl, and Catherine upon Bobby's arrival to the island.
- Chopin's Prelude in E Minor, op. 28, no. 4, played by Dupea for Catherine.
- Mozart's Fantasy in D Minor, K. 397

See Step #76 on creating your iPod playlist. You may want to add these to it for a twist. Variety is always a good thing.

I hope that inspires, motivates, and gets you off the floor.

 WAGON—A piece of exercise equipment that is used in gymnastics alongside the pommel horse.

❊ NEW POINT OF VIEW

Falling off the wagon is no different from dropping an egg on the floor. It's happened to all of us. Now I clean it up and get cookin'! ❊

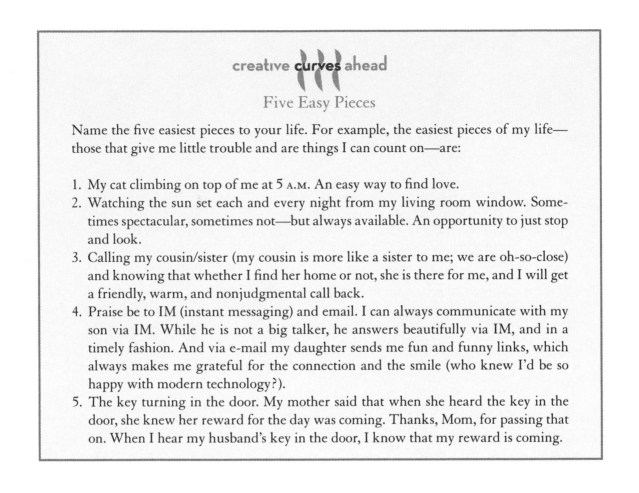

creative curves ahead

Five Easy Pieces

Name the five easiest pieces to your life. For example, the easiest pieces of my life—those that give me little trouble and are things I can count on—are:

1. My cat climbing on top of me at 5 A.M. An easy way to find love.
2. Watching the sun set each and every night from my living room window. Sometimes spectacular, sometimes not—but always available. An opportunity to just stop and look.
3. Calling my cousin/sister (my cousin is more like a sister to me; we are oh-so-close) and knowing that whether I find her home or not, she is there for me, and I will get a friendly, warm, and nonjudgmental call back.
4. Praise be to IM (instant messaging) and email. I can always communicate with my son via IM. While he is not a big talker, he answers beautifully via IM, and in a timely fashion. And via e-mail my daughter sends me fun and funny links, which always makes me grateful for the connection and the smile (who knew I'd be so happy with modern technology?).
5. The key turning in the door. My mother said that when she heard the key in the door, she knew her reward for the day was coming. Thanks, Mom, for passing that on. When I hear my husband's key in the door, I know that my reward is coming.

HOW TO GET AND STAY JAZZED!

Many of us decide to lose weight because we are disgusted, depressed, and in self-hating mode and vow that we are going to do something about it. And you know what? That's not as bad as it sounds. Yes, it's a negative place to be, but at least it has motivated us enough to get off our tushes and do something about those growing rolls of fat.

We find a food plan and we psych ourselves up. Sometimes, we even generate enough electricity to light up Times Square! But as the weeks or months pass, our resolve fades. We have lost the Battle of the Bulge once again.

Creative Act of Weight Loss

Be a 100-watt bulb in a 60-watt world.

HOW TO STAY
PERMANENTLY JAZZED!

Have you ever watched an Olympic swimmer push off the side of the pool? It is quite amaz-ing, isn't it? The thrust, the power, the deter-mination are enormous.

Often the strength of this one solitary push can propel the Olympian right straight to the middle of the Olympic-size pool.

When we decide to go on a "diet," we essentially push off from the side of the pool of discontent. We gather a vast amount of energy from not liking ourselves, being disgusted and ashamed of how we look. We don't like ourselves. No, we sure don't.

Sometimes this energy takes us halfway to our goal weight, sometimes all the way . . . 10, 20, 30, 100, 200 pounds lost. Then what?

Unlike the Olympic swimmer, who has a plan, who is moving toward her big win, who sees herself as a champion and knows with every cell and fiber of her being that she is the victor, we only know ourselves to be losers. We are basing this attempt on past attempts to lose, which have failed.

IT IS EASY TO GET LOST IF YOU DON'T KNOW WHERE YOU ARE GOING

If you want to be victorious at the game of Permanent Fat Removal, then you need to have a compelling future. You need to know where you are going; what you want. The fat does not live alone. This is a holistic event.

HOW TO USE WEIGHT LOSS AS A VEHICLE FOR TRANSFORMATION AND REINVENTION

HAVE A VISION
The root of the word motivation is "motive." The definition of "motive" is "a reason to act."

You need a reason to act. You need both an external and an internal vision of the new you. You need to be moving towards a compelling future! What's your reason to act?

BE PASSIONATE
Motivation is not task-driven. It's all about emotion. It's fire-driven. You've got to fuel your passion (just like you have to fuel your body and fuel your car!). You have to set yourself a goal that connects to an all-consuming desire. What moves you?

STAY FOCUSED
The more focused you are the more results you'll get. The more results, the more motivated you'll be. It's called the "upward spiral." Don't worry about getting dizzy. You're getting lighter and lighter. Keep on spiraling, up, up, up!

BUILD ON YOUR SUCCESSES
If you permanently remove a pound, be proud. When you drop a size, get fired up. Woo hoo! Keep on going!

ACKNOWLEDGE ALL THAT YOU DO WELL
We have a tendency to negate our wins by focusing on the minor slips of the day. If you said "No, thank you" four times, rejoice. What else did you do today that was stupendous? (It could be as simple as filling up a bowl with fresh fruit for the kitchen counter, or filling the room with good energy.)

SEND YOURSELF POSITIVE MESSAGES

Read positive books and listen to good music, anything with an uplifting message. Fill your brain with stories of successful people. It will take hold. Think positive!

Svelte Talk

WINNER—Someone who is on the Rocky Road to Sveltesville, who has a clear vision of where she is going.

JAZZED—A swirling, happy feeling that runs through your body and soul when it is filled with motivation and inspiration rather than processed junk food.

❋ NEW POINT OF VIEW

I am an Olympian. No one removes fat as furiously or efficiently as I do. ❋

---

creative curves ahead

Save any and all inspirational quotes, poems, and stories and create a Motivation Book of your own.

Here's one of my favorite quotes to help get you started:

"Vegetables are sexy, and you can be, too."
—*Our Lady of Weight Loss*

TAKE A MIRACLE DIP

SERVINGS: 8

INGREDIENTS

¼ pound soft tofu
1 tablespoon low sodium soy sauce
2 tablespoons lemon juice
2 scallions, finely chopped
1 teaspoon ground cumin
1 teaspoon turmeric

INSTRUCTIONS

Combine all the ingredients in a blender and process until the mixture is smooth. Transfer it to a bowl and serve it with raw vegetables.

Nutrition Facts

Serving Size (13g)
Servings Per Container 8

Amount Per Serving

Calories 5	Calories from Fat 0

	% Daily Value*
Total Fat 0g	0%
Saturated Fat 0g	0%
Trans Fat 0g	
Cholesterol 0mg	0%
Sodium 70mg	3%
Total Carbohydrate 1g	0%
Dietary Fiber 0g	0%
Sugars 0g	
Protein 0g	

Vitamin A 0%	•	Vitamin C 2%
Calcium 0%	•	Iron 2%

*Percent Daily Values are based on a 2,000 calorie diet. Your daily values may be higher or lower depending on your calorie needs:

	Calories	2,000	2,500
Total Fat	Less Than	65g	80g
Saturated Fat	Less Than	20g	25g
Cholesterol	Less Than	300mg	300 mg
Sodium	Less Than	2,400mg	2,400mg
Total Carbohydrate		300g	375g
Dietary Fiber		25g	30g

Calories per gram:
Fat 9 • Carbohydrate 4 • Protein 4

S$\dagger$N C$\dagger$TY

φ φ φ φ φ φ φ φ φ φ φ φ φ φ φ

The Devil Made Me Do It!

I just ate four Dove Bars!
(And I don't mean the soap.)

YOU are lost in Sin City and the food police have arrested you.

Cash in one of your Get Out of Jail Free cards or wash with Dove soap and go to a peace rally, thus becoming a dove!

Get Out of Jail Free Card

The Sin City food police
have arrested you.

This card may be kept until
needed. It is nontransferable

All is forgiven, move on

STEP 74

ROSIE THE RITUALIST

My friend Felice told me that she incorporated a wonderful morning ritual into her Permanent Fat Removal plan. She lights a candle and says a prayer, and good stuff is beginning to happen to her. She even won money on a slot machine yesterday. And best of all, her eating is under control! There *is* power in the ritual.

RITUALS RULE!

Rituals are a device that allow us to be in touch with all four levels of "being": emotional, mental, physical, and spiritual.

Rituals create an opportunity to take a moment every day to get in touch with the spirit, allowing you to see the world with a new awareness, as a place where a multitude of possibilities exist and where we can see, reach for, and actualize our dreams. This is the space in which we create a purpose-driven life.

By creating a daily ritual, we open the channels between the spirit and the ordinary self. If we quiet ourselves and listen, our spirit will direct and shape our actions for the day, thus restoring balance to our emotions and health. We start the day with good energy, and the "upward spiral" gets set in motion (rather than the downward spiral).

WHAT DOES A RITUAL LOOK LIKE? HERE ARE SOME SAMPLE RITUALS.

DAILY RITUAL: Wake up (hopefully) and pop in a dance DVD. With a cup of coffee in one hand, and a pretend microphone in the other, start your day with a caffeine-enhanced performance. (FYI, a certain amount of caffeine daily is actu-

ally good for you!) Then, look out your living room window and acknowledge that you are happy to be alive. Repeat after me, "I am alive."

FAMILY GATHERING RITUAL: Find a quiet corner in the world (e.g., in a remote part of a public park or beach, or deep in the recesses of your backyard), take in a deep, deep breath, and then scream it out. (Personal confession: My mother lives a block away from the ocean, and on occasion, in the heat of a family gathering, I am wont to slip out, go to the beach, and scream. Are you shocked? I'm just being honest. Saying and doing what some of you might want to do or say—hey?! And for the record, the scream does not diminish my love for them or myself. In fact, it accentuates it!)

WORK RITUAL: When I was working for the man, during break time (or not), I found a moment daily to collage, draw, or write a sentence that expressed the feeling of the day. Sometimes I was actually happy—feeling empowered. And that was a good thing to note. "A+," I wrote on my calendar! And sometimes I was frustrated. Masterpieces may not have been created, but personal expression was released. Ahhh . . . Note: Don't separate your true self from your work self. It's a surefire way to over-order from the ubiquitous take-out menus.

GET IT?

Just like the rest of the ingredients in the Permanent Fat Removal Diet, as long as it's fresh and authentic, it burns fat!

Svelte
Talk

RITUALISTIC OPPORTUNITY—A chance to simultaneously set intention, do a bit of internal exploration, release emotion (e.g., scream), and burn candles.

✳ NEW POINT OF VIEW

Rituals provide a practice in which I can perceive value in the things I already have in my life—from the people in my life to the air I breathe to the sounds I make when screaming. ✳

FORGIVERCIZE
Ritualization

What type of fresh and fat burnin' rituals are you going to put in place?

Name three now! They can be as simple as burning a candle and saying a prayer, doing a cheer in the morning, or flossing your teeth each and every night after dinner to end the night's eating. They're YOUR rituals!

S♆N C♆TY

♆ ♆ ♆ ♆ ♆ ♆ ♆ ♆ ♆ ♆ ♆ ♆ ♆ ♆ ♆

The Devil Made Me Do It!

I lick batter.

YOU are lost in Sin City and the food police have arrested you.

Cash in one of your Get Out of Jail Free cards or go to the batting cage and bat those balls out of the park! (More good exercise as you release stress.)

Get Out of Jail Free Card

The Sin City food police have arrested you.

This card may be kept until needed. It is nontransferable

All is forgiven, move on

STEP 75

THE MOTHER OF ALL MANTRAS

"When women are depressed, they either eat or go shopping.
Men invade another country. It's a whole different way of thinking."
—*Elayne Boosler*

MANTRAS ARE MYSTICAL, MAGICAL, AND TRANSFORMATIONAL

A mantra is a religious or mystical syllable, poem, word, or series of words that is chanted aloud or silently. Mantras can be used for a variety of life tasks and create a space for transformational opportunities. When chanted, mantras become vibrations that establish one-pointed concentration in the person chanting. They are, in one sense, the most ancient method of using affirmations to bring about changes in your life.

Translated, the word "mantra" means "that which when reflected upon gives liberation." Each mantra calls upon a specific power, which can be used for a particular purpose: spiritual growth, psychic healing, physical healing, prosperity, Permanent Fat Removal. When the mantra is chanted with great intention and commitment, the mantra can become that much more empowering.

THE PRACTICAL APPLICATION OF THE MANTRA IN PERMANENT FAT REMOVAL

There are those who think that the doughnut magically and mysteriously jumped into their mouth, all on its own. Sorry to say, doughnuts can't jump. Perhaps said doughnut eaters were semiunconscious, busy talking to someone else while their hands were reaching for the little buggers, but there you have it. They put the doughnuts in their mouth.

When it comes to Permanent Fat Removal, the mantra creates a pause between you and the doughnut. It is a tool that provides enough time and space to stop you from eating the doughnut.

MANTRAS PROVIDE A MOMENT OF SELF-AWARENESS

If you consistently repeat your mantra when you see food that you are tempted to eat, you will establish a worthwhile habit.

Be sure to chant your Permanent Fat Removal mantra with love, intention, and commitment. Be strong. Create a pause. Your initial reaction to the visual stimuli will pass.

Here are some samples of mantras that have worked for others. It is a very personal thing. Make sure you pick a mantra that means something special to you and resonates deeply with your "thinner core."

Keep in mind that mantras increase in power in direct relation to the number of times the mantra is chanted. And it is said by those who are in the know about such matters that after the user (that's you) chants her mantra 125,000 times, the mantra is fully empowered by becoming "seated" in the heart. The technical term for this is Mantra Siddhi. Wow! That's a lot of mantra.

SAMPLE MANTRAS

Want power • Baby steps • Face it • I'm responsible for what goes in my mouth • In the groove • I remain conscious • Feel the power • I'm already there • Love power

Or you can chant a more traditional form:

Om Sri Ram Jai Ram Jai Jai Ram
(used by Swami Ramdas)

Translation:
Om: the expression of the whole of being, of the ultimate creative energy in the universe
Sri: a title of honor
Ram: lord
Jai: hail!

Om Tare Tutare Ture Soha
(used by the female Buddha, Tara)

Translation:

Om: the cosmic sound that keeps us together.

Tare: the feminine aspect of compassion that resides within all sentient creatures in the universe

Ture: the seed syllables that activate the center of compassion within us.

Soha: may the meaning of the mantra take root in my mind.

Svelte Talk

MANTRA—That which, when reflected upon, gives liberation from food thoughts, thus creating an opening for exploration of the other senses.

❊ NEW POINT OF VIEW

My mantra gives me pause for thought and creates a pathway to freedom. ❊

FORGIVERCISE
Chant on!

What's your mantra?

The practice of chanting a mantra is considered the easiest form of meditation. Sit comfortably. Close your eyes. Take in a deep cleansing breath and let it out. Relax. Allow your mind to focus on your mantra (one that you've created or one of the above). Now chant it either aloud or to yourself.

JAMMIN' TO THE BEAT OF METALLICA

"Let your head be more than a funnel to your stomach."
—German proverb

Jammin' Joanne, a good friend of Our Lady of Weight Loss, was telling me that music helps her to lose weight. She said, "You know, I'm not a teenager [actually, she's sixty-seven], but I love jammin' on my drums to Metallica or ZZ Top! I play the piano as well, and I can say with certainty that when I'm pounding away, I don't even think of those cookies that are in my kitchen. I consider jammin' on my drums to be an excellent creative act of weight loss—and good exercise." She then flexed her arm muscles—whoa! Get me a set of drums!

Jammin' Joanne got me to thinking about the magic of music—the exciting dance that it initiates within the brain between the cerebral cortex and the limbic system, the site of human feelings. This emotional interplay is set into motion by the hypothalamus, from which feelings of pleasure, relaxation, fear, aggression, and rage originate.

The hypothalamus also controls body tem-

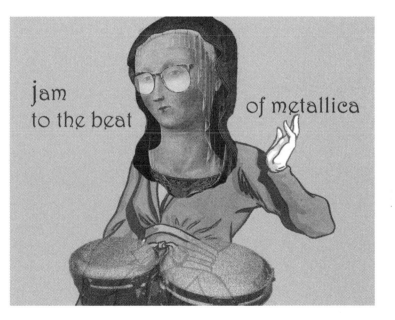

jam to the beat of metallica

perature, hunger, thirst, and circadian cycles (a roughly twenty-four-hour cycle in the physiological processes of living beings).

185

Studies suggest that music releases endorphins and has a therapeutic effect. Endorphins dull pain and affect emotions.

To tap into this phenomenon, you can play or perform music that matches your emotional state (dreary?), gradually introducing cheerier music to create a happy and energized state. Or you can go straight to music that energizes and enlivens, creating an emotional jump start.

Different types of music can also help to boost concentration, bring forth mental clarity, get your sexual juices flowing, or mellow you out.

HOW TO CREATE YOUR OWN PLAYLIST

In order for music to enhance your state of mind, you need to like the music. In other words, there is no magic-bullet playlist that will melt your melancholy mood or remove your excess weight.

Here's what to do. You be the music doctor! Make a list of twenty or so songs that you respond to. Rate them on a scale from zero to ten (zero being soul-crushing and ten being ecstasy). When you need to lift your mood, which will certainly keep you away from the cookies, tune in!

Svelte Talk

MUSICOLOGY—The art of arranging sounds to create a rather dramatic and unexpectedly stimulating and fat-burnin' effect that sets the hypothalamus into overdrive.

✳ NEW POINT OF VIEW

Music activates the same feel-good center of the brain that food does, and it motivates and helps me to burn fat, too. I'm blowin' my own mind! ✳

creative curves ahead

Burn a CD of Your Favorite Music

I spent hours and hours putting together a CD of my favorite "food" walking music. I wanted to keep to the food theme, because it reminds me that food isn't just for eating! I've changed my relationship with food. Now, when I hear the words "lime" or "coconut," I start to boogie!

My playlist consists of:
(Put the Lime in the) Coconut
Cabbage Rolls and Coffee (a great polka)
Mambo Italiano
Okra
She Don't Use Jelly
Breakfast Power
That's Amore

SPICED TEA

SERVINGS: 8

INGREDIENTS

Lemon peel from one lemon
Orange peel from one orange
3 cardamom pods
2 whole star anise pods
6 cups boiling water
3 tablespoons green tea

INSTRUCTIONS

1. Put the lemon peel, orange peel, cardamom, and star anise pods into a tea ball.
2. Blend the boiling water with the tea and drop in the tea ball containing the spice mixture. Infuse for 10 minutes.

Tea may be served hot or cold.

Nutrition Facts		
Serving Size (241g)		
Servings Per Container 8		
Amount Per Serving		
Calories 5	Calories from Fat 0	
		% Daily Value*
Total Fat 0g		0%
Saturated Fat 0g		0%
Trans Fat 0g		
Cholesterol 0mg		0%
Sodium 0mg		0%
Total Carbohydrate 1g		0%
Dietary Fiber 0g		0%
Sugars 0g		
Protein 0g		
Vitamin A 0%	•	Vitamin C 8%
Calcium 0%	•	Iron 0%

*Percent Daily Values are based on a 2,000 calorie diet. Your daily values may be higher or lower depending on your calorie needs:

	Calories	2,000	2,500
Total Fat	Less Than	65g	80g
Saturated Fat	Less Than	20g	25g
Cholesterol	Less Than	300mg	300 mg
Sodium	Less Than	2,400mg	2,400mg
Total Carbohydrate		300g	375g
Dietary Fiber		25g	30g

Calories per gram:
Fat 9 • Carbohydrate 4 • Protein 4

SIN CITY

The Devil Made Me Do It!

*I read that blue food makes people lose their appetites.
So I dyed all my food blue. That was kind of fun . . .
But when it came time to eat, I put on my rose-colored glasses . . .
and blew it.*

YOU are lost in Sin City and the food police have arrested you.

Cash in one of your Get Out of Jail Free cards or throw out the rose-colored glasses and get real. And while you are at it, buy ALL IS FORGIVEN, move on Blue wristbands from Our Lady of Weight Loss (www.ourladyofweightloss.com)!

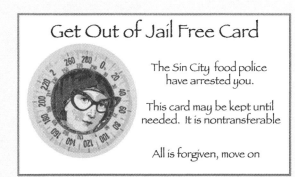

Get Out of Jail Free Card

The Sin City food police
have arrested you.

This card may be kept until
needed. It is nontransferable

All is forgiven, move on

FASHION STOP 78

ROSE-COLORED GLASSES

Speaking of rose-colored glasses, you absolutely must visit Fabulous Fanny's, on East Ninth Street in New York's East Village, for the best vintage eyewear ever. Tell Ken and Stan that Our Lady of Weight Loss sent you!

They have an online presence (www. fabulousfannys.com), and while you can find some awesome eyewear there, you really need to go to the store for the full impact. Not only are there hundreds of pairs of vintage and new eyeglasses to choose from, Ken and Stan and the rest of the crew are the nicest peeps ever. FYI . . . Stan can add rhinestones to anything!

It's worth a visit to New York just for the eyewear.

Let me know if you're in town. I'll go with you!

STEP 79

YOUR *NOT* TO DO LIST

People often ask me, "How do you do it all?" To which I respond, "What makes you think I do it all? I don't. I can't remember the last time I cleaned, for goodness' sake."

Here's how to clear your calendar. Draw a line down the center of a piece of paper. On one side of the paper write "to do," and then on the other side of the page write "not to do." Now, write out all you have to do on the "to do" side of the page. We really do have ridiculously long "to do" lists, don't we?

Here comes the fun part! Take a good look at your "to do" list and take anything on it that someone else could do for you and move it to your "not to do" list. For instance, take the laundry. Either find someone else in the house who is capable of tossing it into the washer and drier or send it out. Is food shopping taking up too much of your precious time? Order online or call in a standing delivery to your neighborhood grocery store. Cleaning? Forgetaboutit.

Our Lady of Weight Loss

Creative Act of Weight Loss
polish your tiara

I'm lucky. My husband has a much lower tolerance for mess than I do. I can count on him to clean up!

A quick review: Thus far, you've received an advanced degree in dieting, and you've got to be feeling fairly accomplished! You are laughing it up while you are slimming down. You have forgiven and will continue to forgive your dietary transgressions. And you've cleared your calendar and now have time to do the things that make your heart sing! You get it, right? Laughing, having fun, and feeling accomplished all lay the groundwork for a clear and positive foundation for you to move forward on. Foundation is everything! (I love MAC's foundation.)

You're lightening up, aren't you? Feel it!

Svelte Talk

FOUNDATION—A positive, low-fat, low-cal, vegetable-and-fruit-stocked framework on which you build your compelling future (as well as something for you to schmear on your cheeks).

❈ NEW POINT OF VIEW

Do NOT do it all! ❈

STEP 80

THE MULTIPLEX OF THINGS TO DO

NOW that you've cleared your calendar and created some time for yourself, pull off to the side of the road and find a nice tree to sit under—preferably a weeping willow. Feel the air, take in a good cleansing breath, breathe out, and with pen in hand, write a long list of the things you like to do. Don't think too hard. Just write.

SUCCULENT SUGGESTIONS FOR FREE-TIME SCENARIOS

Go to the movies alone. (You can go into a quiet, happy state and escape the stress and challenges of the day without being concerned as to whether or not the person with you is enjoying the movie.)

Take a square dancing class.
Sit in the park.

Faith is a journey, not a guilt trip.

Go to a museum.

Take a road trip (of another nature).

Write a short story or even a novel.

Paint.

Sing.

Bird watch.

Take a healthy cooking class.

Take a belly dancing class.

Go thrift-store shopping.

Buy a hat.

Listen to stories on the radio. (A flashback to the old days—before my time, for the record!)

Go the hairdresser (even if it's just for a wash and blow!).

Spy on your neighbors with binoculars. (Just kidding!)

Visit www.craftychica.com for tons of fun ideas.

Svelte Talk

AIR—A substance that we breathe, but more importantly feel. *(Take a moment; feel it on your cheeks and arms.)*

❋ NEW POINT OF VIEW

Permanent Fat Removal is about feeding myself the things that I like to do, and in so doing, feeding my soul. ❋

Fat Lib . . .

Remember silly ol' Mad Libs? They are kind of dumb but fun!

It's easy to write your own, too. Here's mine! Go ahead . . . give it a go! It's a fun activity with friends. You see, it's not all about eating. It's about sharing!

The Movies

The movies are always fun to visit on a hot summer's _____ (*noun—period of time*). When you get there, you can buy something to _____ (*action verb*) or _____ (*action verb*). You can start off with a/an _____ (*adjective*) _____ (*noun*) with _____ (*condiment*) or a _____ (*adjective*) of _____ (*size*) _____ (*food item*).

Or you bring your own fat-free _____ (*food item*). A piece of _____ (*noun*) is a good idea, too. And a bottle of _____ (*liquid*)!

After the movie, you might want to take a _____ (*action verb*) and burn off whatever _____ (*noun*) you ingested.

"E" STOP 81

JUGGLE OR JIGGLE!

"Food has replaced sex in my life. Now I can't even get into my own pants."
—Anonymous

IN NEED OF AN EXERCISE PLAN?
CONSIDER JUGGLING . . .

Juggling is a highly aerobic activity, a very cool way to exercise.

The repetitive motion of juggling builds muscles that aren't ordinarily used in our daily lives. Jugglers are generally fit, lean, and muscular. (Sounds good to me.)

Juggling also exercises your brain and develops hand-eye coordination. All the skills that you learn from juggling are transferable and can be applied to other sports!

The repetitive patterns take concentration and can help to relieve you of stress. It's a kind of meditation. Jugglers have described going into a state of bliss and tranquility.

Juggling takes time to learn, but it's well worth it. You can do it almost anywhere; it's inexpensive; it's noncompetitive; and age doesn't matter. Juggling is a great confidence builder, and rest assured, you'll be the life of the party.

A LITTLE JUGGLING HISTORY

During medieval times, jugglers traveled throughout Europe, from town to town, performing their juggling tricks for money. And the English were so into it that they gave their top juggler a title—King of Jugglers—and he (or she?) would perform juggling tricks for the royals!

By the time the twentieth century rolled around, jugglers had developed different styles and performed their tricks with clubs, guns, chairs, and cannonballs.

I'm going to give it a juggle.

And you?

Svelte Talk

JUGGLE—An opportunity to keep adjusting your grip (on whatever you are tossing up into the air, whether it's balls, bats, or life in general) while remaining in a balanced state.

❋ NEW POINT OF VIEW

No more jiggle for me! If all else fails, I'll have a backup career! I'll join the circus! ❋

STEP 82

APPETITE COLORS!

*"Somewhere over the rainbow, skies are blue, and the dreams
that you dare to dream really do come true."*
—*E. Y. Harburg*

I am sure that you are aware that there are warm colors and cool colors—but did you know that there are appetite colors? There are! Something you will surely want to be aware of as you travel to Sveltesville.

COLOR IS MYSTICAL AND MAGICAL

Color communicates with our emotions. Color inspires, energizes, soothes, and enlivens, and color affects our appetite.

WARM COLORS radiate the fiery tones of sunlight and create a feeling of warmth in a room. They promote conversation and personal interaction. Cozy!

COOL COLORS tend to have a calming effect. They can feel comforting and nurturing. Good colors to relax with are lavender, ocean blue, and forest green—all colors of nature.

AND THEN THERE ARE THE APPETITE COLORS
Food colors can lessen our appetites! Blue is by far the most popular color, but it is absolutely the least appetizing. Some weight-loss plans suggest putting your food on a blue plate.

But if you really want to leave a trail of fat behind you (oops, be careful that no one falls), you'll want to take it a step or two further!

THE MAGIC LIGHT SHOW

There may be no magic bullet, but try putting a blue light in your refrigerator, as well as in your dining room. And . . . dye your food blue.

Why? Blue food is rare in nature. Aside from blueberries and blue-purple potatoes, blue foods don't exist in any significant quantity. There are no blue leafy vegetables or blue meats that I know of. A million years ago, when early humans were out foraging for food, they learned that blue, purple, and black were "col-

ors of warning" of potentially deadly food. Therefore, we don't have an automatic appetite response to blue food. We may even have a built-in, primal avoidance.

So paint your safe corner or room a cool color so that you can chill, and dye all your food blue! Now that's food for thought!

Svelte Talk
BLUE PLATE PHENOMENON— Dinnerware in varying shades of blue that mysteriously causes one to lose her appetite. Perfect for those who want to limit their intake of food. The darker the blue the better.

❋ NEW POINT OF VIEW
Color all red-light foods blue! ❋

All Is
Forgiven,
Move On

199

creative **curves** ahead

You've heard of "go green"? Creating an eco-friendly environment? Well, Our Lady of Weight Loss says, "Go blue!"

OUR LADY OF WEIGHT LOSS'S BLUE INITIATIVE!

A Half Dozen Ways to "Go Blue"

1. Add blue food dye to your food.
2. Put a blue light in your refrigerator.
3. Serve dinner on dark blue dinnerware.
4. Drink from dark blue tumblers.
5. Make your dining room a blue-light district. Paint the walls blue and use blue light bulbs.
6. Wear blue-tinted sunglasses.

BLUE ON BLUEBERRY COBBLER

SERVINGS: 6

INGREDIENTS

6 cups fresh blueberries
2 teaspoons dried rosemary
2 tablespoons light brown sugar
2 cups whole-wheat flour, plus more for dusting kneading
surface
⅛ teaspoon kosher salt
2 teaspoons baking powder
2 teaspoons butter
2 tablespoons fat free sour cream
¼ cup skim milk

INSTRUCTIONS

1. Preheat oven 400°F.
2. Arrange the blueberries in a 9 x 13" baking dish. Sprinkle them
with the rosemary and sugar.

Nutrition Facts

Serving Size (186g)
Servings Per Container 6

Amount Per Serving

Calories 180	Calories from Fat 20

% Daily Value*

Total Fat 2g	3%
Saturated Fat 1g	5%
Trans Fat 0g	
Cholesterol 5mg	2%
Sodium 170mg	7%
Total Carbohydrate 40g	13%
Dietary Fiber 6g	24%
Sugars 18g	
Protein 5g	

Vitamin A 4%	•	Vitamin C 25%
Calcium 6%	•	Iron 6%

*Percent Daily Values are based on a 2,000 calorie diet. Your daily values may be higher or lower depending on your calorie needs:

	Calories	2,000	2,500
Total Fat	Less Than	65g	80g
Saturated Fat	Less Than	20g	25g
Cholesterol	Less Than	300mg	300 mg
Sodium	Less Than	2,400mg	2,400mg
Total Carbohydrate		300g	375g
Dietary Fiber		25g	30g

Calories per gram:
Fat 9 • Carbohydrate 4 • Protein 4

3. In a bowl, stir together the flour, salt, and baking powder.
4. In another bowl, combine the butter and sour cream. Add the butter mixture to the flour mixture and stir in the milk.
5. Transfer the dough to a lightly floured surface and knead the dough until it is smooth. Roll out the dough to ¼" thickness.
6. Cut the dough into 1" wide strips and arrange them on top of the blueberries at ¼" intervals
7. Bake the cobbler for 30 minutes or until the blueberries are bubbly and the dough is golden brown.

Janice
Taylor

S**I**N C**I**TY

ψ ψ ψ ψ ψ ψ ψ ψ ψ ψ ψ ψ ψ ψ ψ ψ ψ

The Devil Made Me Do It!

I was delirious from the heat and downed a two-liter bottle of cola,
fully loaded. Sugar . . . caffeine.
Ahhh . . . what a buzz.

YOU are lost in Sin City and the food police have arrested you.

Cash in one of your Get Out of Jail Free cards or brew up and drink a
few gallons of decaffeinated tea, straight up (no sugar or sweetener of
any kind). Cleanse thyself!

Get Out of Jail Free Card

The Sin City food police
have arrested you.

This card may be kept until
needed. It is nontransferable

All is forgiven, move on

STEP 84

STOPPING MECHANISM

When I was a baby, my mother and father fed me until I could eat no more. "Really, no more, please!" I cried.

But to no avail. They were so happy feeding me that they mistook the "stop" cry for the "more" cry.

But what could I do? I mean, really. I was just a little baby, and even then, I was apt to please. So I opened my miniature mouth, and in came the "aer-o-plane," bringing with it another spoonful of Mother's delicious, maple syrup–enhanced butternut squash puree.

Charming and inventive baby that I was, I came up with a system to store the excess pulverized pulp in my cheeks.

My parents squealed with delight as my cheeks puffed rounder and fuller until they were so fully packed, one more spoonful would have caused me to burst. I then slowly swallowed the puree bit by bit.

I puffed and they cooed to me and to each other. "Honey, she looks like a capuchin monkey," Father said.

"Or a blowfish," replied Mother.

As you can well see and understand, I never did get in touch with that "I'm full. Don't have to eat it all, plus some. That's enough. I'm done. No more, thanks." feeling.

As I continued through life, I no longer stored food in my cheeks, but I continued to overeat. I didn't stop eating until my heart was racing and breathing was troublesome—until I was about ready to burst!

So, as I traversed the Rocky Road to Sveltesville, it was natural for me to wonder (as you might wonder now), how to find a natural stopping place. I asked myself, "If the number one signifies emptiness, hunger, and the number ten represents a state of being overstuffed, where between one and ten might I find a comfortable place to stop?"

I thought about the number 5, and while it is midway along the scale, I thought I might like to feel fuller than 5. The numbers 6 and 7 felt comfortable. I wanted to create a place of satisfaction where I would be left feeling sated. Since each day is different from the next, I decided on a range: 5, 6, and 7. Yes, stopping at 5, 6, or 7, or even 6 and a quarter, would be fine.

And so I closed my eyes (as you can do now) and imagined in my mind's eye a pendulum swinging—back and forth, back and forth—above the numbers 1 through 10.

The numbers—one through ten—are floating consecutively from left to right, evenly spaced apart. The numbers 5, 6, and 7 appear to be a bit larger and are in boldface. Those three numbers are magnetically charged. And when the pendulum swings—back and forth—over those numbers, it can't help but slow as it is pulled to pause over the 6—or perhaps the 7 or even the 5—and consider its position.

In this new place, the pendulum's mesmerizing power grows and strengthens, holding steady. The magnetic field reminds us that we are full—satisfied, sated. Sated with the right amount of healthy foods—and filled with joy and sunshine; with the enjoyment of a good read or a great movie; with friendship and laughter—you feel full. You are full.

It's exciting to know that you have the power to feel sated and full of love and happiness available at any time, isn't it? Now, when you pick up a fork, a knife, a spoon, a cup, or a plate—an eating utensil of any kind—or food of any kind, you will remember that you have this wonderful, magical, lucky number that floats gently through your body and mind, leaving you feeling sated.

From now on, you eat to sustain yourself—you "eat to live." You now receive enjoyment, satisfaction, love, and happiness from many places and things.

Svelte Talk

COMFORT FOOD—Food that satisfies and brings you to a relaxed place and neither stuffs you nor leaves you feeling empty.

❋ NEW POINT OF VIEW

I know when to stop—and if I don't, I will install my own stopping mechanism, a true Creative Act of Weight Loss! ❋

STEP 85

PERMISSION TO SLIP

"I do whatever my Rice Krispies tell me to."
—*author unknown*

OUR LADY OF WEIGHT LOSS IS GIVING YOU PERMISSION TO GIVE YOURSELF PERMISSION TO BE YOURSELF!

I hear from lots of frustrated artists, crafters, bowlers, creative types, and the like, saying that they just don't have time to write, sing, paint, sew, or even ride their horses, because they're too busy doing all the things they are supposed to do. By the time night rolls around, they're exhausted. Instead of feeding their souls, they feed their tummies with all kinds of non–Our Lady of Weight Loss–approved snacks.

They ask me, "How do you do it? How do you find the time to take care of your family, write, make art, sing, walk, and talk?"

Okay, here's my secret. My best energy is in the morning. So I basically work on all my creative projects in the morning. It's fabulous to wake up to something you want to do! And truly, does one need to be fully awake to vacuum? Does it matter how much dust I miss? And if we run out of clean underwear, we can always run to the corner store and buy an extra pair or two! In the end, all the things that have to get done do get done. But if you put yourself last, you'll never get to it!

It's important to give yourself permission to take care of yourself, first and foremost, before all others. You might think this a selfish act, but truly, if you are running on empty, how can you help someone else?

When flying (on an airplane, not when taking flights of fancy), does not the flight attendant caution you to put the oxygen mask on yourself first, and then on your child? If you're out of oxygen, what good are you?

Life works in the same way. The more fulfilled and happy you are, the more you'll be able to give. That is a fact.

Our loved ones take cues from our behavior. If we are constantly putting ourselves on the back burner, we are teaching others to treat us in the same way. (Believe me. No one in my house expects to find everything in order when they return home at the end of the day.)

If we don't take care of ourselves and take ourselves seriously, why should they?

Svelte Talk **PERMISSION**—An agreement you make with yourself that allows you to be your authentic self.

✳ NEW POINT OF VIEW

I now have permission to slip, slide, smile, and stand! ✳

creative **curves** ahead

PERMISSION SLIP
(for those in need of permission)

I understand that giving myself permission to do any and all of the following involves a certain degree of risk. I just might break out and be who I always dreamed of being. (Whoa! That's scary!)

I hereby give myself permission to act silly, giggle, chortle, snigger and titter.

I hereby give myself permission to see the absurdity and humor in any and all of life's happenings.

I hereby give myself permission to take time to engage in activities that replenish my soul, e.g., walk, talk, finger paint, learn a new language, play an instrument, travel the globe.

I hereby give myself permission to daydream, fantasize, and contemplate my navel.

I hereby give myself permission to nap—daily—for a period of not less than ten minutes.

I hereby give myself permission to spend time with my thoughts, be in touch with my feelings, sing that awful song "feelings, whoa feelings," and say nice things to myself about myself.

I hereby give myself permission to take in deep cleansing breaths, stretch, shake it out, and sing in and out of the shower.

I hereby give myself permission to take care of myself before all others. I know there are family members, coworkers, neighbors depending upon me, but I realize that if I don't take care of myself first, I won't have anything to give.

All Is
Forgiven,
Move On

It is duly noted that it is riskier not to take a risk than to take one. I understand that if I GET OUT THERE, take a LEAP OF FAITH, and GO FOR IT, I am far more likely to reach my goals, conquer my fears, and create my dreams.

I, _____, have carefully considered the risk involved and hereby give full support, consent, and permission to MYSELF to fully participate in life, bust out of the box, be joyous, and go for my dream on this _____ day of _____, in the year two thousand _____.

Signed by:

_____

Name (signature)

_____

Name (please print)   Date

_____

Our Lady of Weight Loss is with you every ounce of the "weigh."

FASHION STOP 86

PERMISSION SLIP

What can I say? More high fashion from Our Lady of Weight Loss. She's a fashionista with a sense of humor. We're working on a line of clothing!

INSTRUCTIONS

Ask yourself: What things do I want to do and accomplish? Where do I want to go that I haven't been able to give myself permission to go? Then write out all those things. Put them on heat-transfer paper and iron them onto a half-slip!

S✝N C✝TY

♈ ♈ ♈ ♈ ♈ ♈ ♈ ♈ ♈ ♈ ♈ ♈ ♈ ♈

The Devil Made Me Do It!

In need of a sugar fix,
I sucked all the ketchup out of its premeasured plastic wrapper.

YOU are lost in Sin City and the food police have arrested you.

Cash in one of your Get Out of Jail Free cards or give yourself permission to enjoy one sugar treat per week, so you do not have to suck ketchup!

Get Out of Jail Free Card

The Sin City food police have arrested you.

This card may be kept until needed. It is nontransferable

All is forgiven, move on

"E" STOP 87

EXERCISE YOUR BRAIN

"If it wasn't for wrestling with my conscience . . . I'd get no exercise at all."
—Tom Wilson in *It's Not Will Power I Need . . .*

IT'S TIME TO REVITALIZE YOUR BRAIN CIRCUITS!

As the natural aging process progresses, our mental and physical functions can, in time, become impaired.

How to slow this process?

In addition to a well balanced and healthful diet and physical exercise, neurobics can aid the antiaging process.

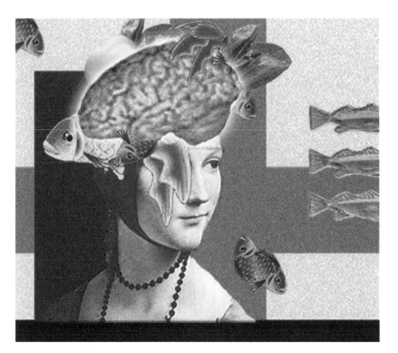

creative curves ahead

Here are some fun neurobic exercises.

- Upon waking, use your nondominant hand as you comb your hair, get dressed, brush your teeth, or make coffee.

- Close your eyes as you shower and use your sense of touch to locate your soap and wash yourself.

- Pair an odor with a specific task. Sniff mint leaves while calling your mother, to help you remember the number.

- Play "smell and tell." Have friends or family members close their eyes, sniff an aroma held under their nose, and tell you what it is that they are smelling.

- Turn the pictures on your desk or shelves upside down. Or better yet, turn your friend's or coworker's photos upside down and see how long it takes them to notice it.

- Rearrange your living room furniture before anyone gets home from school or the office. Watch their befuddled faces!

- Take a different route to work or shopping.

- Eat a meal with your family in silence. Use only visual cues. (Alternatively, if they insist on speaking, wear earplugs.)

- Listen to music while you smell the roses (or the flower of your choice).

- Take your child, life partner, or parent to work with you for the day. (Did you hear that, kids? I'm coming to work with you!)

Wow, I'm exhausted. I strengthened the synapses between my nerve cells, and now my brain cells are busy making growth molecules. Technically speaking, it takes energy to fire those neurons. I wonder how many calories I burned.

Svelte Talk

NATURAL AGING PROCESS—The process of changing with time, in accordance with the usual course of nature, which we artificially change through any means made available.

❋ NEW POINT OF VIEW

I can lift a 250-pound dumbbell with my brain! I am a class A neurobicizer! ❋

STOP
FUEL
38

HOW-TO-THINK-LIKE-A-STRING-BEAN
GREEN BEANS

SERVINGS: 6

INGREDIENTS

2 quarts water
1 tablespoon kosher salt
1 pound green beans, trimmed
1½ teaspoons olive oil
¼ cup chopped shallots
1 garlic clove, peeled and minced
1 cup chopped tomato (such as Pomi)
1 tablespoon balsamic vinegar
1 can (14 oz) artichokes in water, drained and quartered
1 teaspoon vanilla extract
1 tablespoon Italian parsley, finely chopped

INSTRUCTIONS

1. Bring the water to a boil and add the salt. Add the green beans and cook them for 1 minute. Remove the green beans from the hot water and shock them in ice water or rinse them under very cold water. Drain them and set them aside

Nutrition Facts		
Serving Size (493g)		
Servings Per Container 6		
Amount Per Serving		
Calories 310	Calories from Fat 20	
		% Daily Value*
Total Fat 2g		3%
Saturated Fat 0g		0%
Trans Fat 0g		
Cholesterol 0mg		0%
Sodium 550mg		23%
Total Carbohydrate 54g		18%
Dietary Fiber 13g		52%
Sugars 7g		
Protein 20g		
Vitamin A 10%	•	Vitamin C 25%
Calcium 10%	•	Iron 35%

*Percent Daily Values are based on a 2,000 calorie diet. Your daily values may be higher or lower depending on your calorie needs:

	Calories	2,000	2,500
Total Fat	Less Than	65g	80g
Saturated Fat	Less Than	20g	25g
Cholesterol	Less Than	300mg	300 mg
Sodium	Less Than	2,400mg	2,400mg
Total Carbohydrate		300g	375g
Dietary Fiber		25g	30g

Calories per gram:
Fat 9 • Carbohydrate 4 • Protein 4

2. Heat a large sauté pan over medium heat. Once it is heated, add the olive oil, the shallots, and garlic and stir. Cook them for 1–2 minutes or until the shallots become translucent.
3. Add the chopped tomatoes to the pan, along with the balsamic vinegar, beans, and artichokes.
4. Bring the mixture to a boil and return it to a simmer. Cook for 10 minutes.
5. Just before serving, add the vanilla extract and stir. Garnish with the parsley.

All Is
Forgiven,
Move On

217

SIN CITY

🔱 🔱 🔱 🔱 🔱 🔱 🔱 🔱 🔱 🔱 🔱 🔱 🔱 🔱 🔱

The Devil Made Me Do It!

I own a rowing machine, a treadmill, a stationary bike, a real bike,
a StairMaster, a ThighMaster!—enough equipment to start my own gym!
But nevertheless, I joined the most expensive health club ever . . .
and here I sit, watching television, munching on chips.

YOU are lost in Sin City and the food police have arrested you.

Cash in one of your Get Out of Jail Free cards or be honest with yourself and find a new way to move and shake your body that is enjoyable
to you! (See "E" Stop #34, page 84.)

Get Out of Jail Free Card

The Sin City food police
have arrested you.

This card may be kept until
needed. It is nontransferable

All is forgiven, move on

STEP 89

STOP! AND SMELL THE ROSES

CREATIVE ACT OF WEIGHT LOSS

STOP

and smell the roses

Since 75 percent of what we experience as taste comes from our sense of smell, I thought that I'd conduct my own personal experiment. And when a craving came crashing through—and oh, boy, did it!—I'd go smell something fabulous and see if the craving would pass. And more often than not, it did!

The olfactory experience is the most overlooked of all our senses.

Odor molecules enter the passage between

the nose and mouth. Whether we smell appealing aromas, such as those from certain flowers, or rank odors, such as those from rotting garbage, we have specific behavioral responses to the smells.

We might take in a deep breath and smile wide or cover our noses and hold our breath!

I'm in favor of taking in a deep breath, followed by a big sigh. Essential oils are often used to create a relaxed ambience within the home.

HOW TO USE ESSENTIAL OILS

One of the best delivery systems to scent the air, support the atmosphere, and support a meditative state is a diffuser.

Add six to eight drops of your favorite scent to water in a diffuser or place the drops directly into a bowl of boiling water.

Add ten to twenty drops of undiluted essential oil to the water unit of a vaporizer or humidifier.

You can make your own aromatherapy spray. Mix half a cup of distilled water with forty to sixty drops of essential oil in a glass or plastic spray bottle. Shake well before spraying.

Place cotton wool balls fragranced with lavender in drawers and linen closets to deter moths.

Put four drops of oil onto a cotton wool ball and place it behind the heater or radiator in winter.

Put a drop or two of oil onto a cold lightbulb in a lamp so the fragrance fills the room as the bulb heats up.

Candles fragranced with essential oil can also be used to give the home a pleasant ambience and aroma.

Svelte Talk   **OLFACTORY SENSE**—A readily available weapon in the Battle of the Bulge.

✳ NEW POINT OF VIEW

I can fill my stomach with delicious aromas! ✳

creative **curves** ahead

Visit the various perfume counters at a major department store and ask for samples. You can collect enough little vials to last you at least two years! Or tie them up with a pretty bow and some raffia and give as gifts! Bonus: You're walking, talking, and burning calories while collecting free stuff. What could be better?

STEP 90

GO MONOCHROMATIC!

"I wish my butt did not go sideways, but I guess I have to face that."
—Christie Brinkley

WHAT TO DO WHEN
YOU HIT A PLATEAU

GO MONOCHROME!

No kidding. Hitting a plateau—depending on how long you are waylaid—can be dispiriting.

I hit a four-week plateau after I'd lost close to 40 pounds. The scale wasn't budging, and I really wanted to permanently remove just a couple more pounds. So rather than go postal, I went mono. Monochromatic, that is.

For a longer and leaner look, wear just one color from head to toe. And if you wear black from head to toe, you'll look down right bony.

SOME MORE TRICKS FOR THE FASHIONISTA IN YOU

Color

Two colors break the body in half (ouch), but if you insist, be sure to wear the darker color on the bottom.

To add a layer of interest (not fat), try a nice mix of textures. Cashmere, suede, velvet, soft wool—delicious!

An alternative to the above is to blend different shades of the same color. Brown, coffee, and chocolate, or grey, slate, and charcoal—keeping the lighter shades on top!

The blouse

Deep-six the ruffles, would you? Especially if you are a large-breasted gal.

The skirt

Make sure it is longer than it is wide! Fuller skirts definitely look better longer; straight skirts lend themselves to a shorter length. However, alert! Very long skirts can be aging. Steer clear of pleats. They add pounds! Hemlines should hit the narrowest part of the calf. Wear wrap-around skirts to effectively camouflage bulging stomach, hips, and tush. A wrap coat can also make you look thinner.

The jacket

Single-breasted is better than double! No hidden pockets. No belts or bulky pockets. Nothing whatsoever to draw attention to the midriff. Got it? Especially if your midriff is your "area of challenge."

THE PANTS

Wide-bottom pants widen (duh)! Well-cut, tailored, straight-legged pants are best, and again, no bulky or hidden pockets, please.

THE HOSIERY

Wear hosiery the same color as your shoes. And how about those control-top panty hose? And Spanx, of course! Is that a great invention, or what? Five pounds instantly gone!

THE BELT

Tight belts can cause bulging. You are forewarned!

THE SHOES

Sling-back and backless shoes, rather than pumps, make your legs look longer and thinner.

Svelte Talk

SHOPPING TROLLEY (NOT TO BE CONFUSED WITH SHOPPING TROLLOP)—The UK version of a shopping cart in which to place your valuable monochromatic finds.

❋ NEW POINT OF VIEW

I wear clothes that fit!

Now that I'm feeling all svelte, thin, and slim in my ruffle-free, belt-free, monochromatic outfit, I'm able to withstand a plateau or two. It's part of the journey—and a good reason to shop! (I recommend bluefly.com for at-home, online shopping.) ❋

SIN CITY

ψ ψ ψ ψ ψ ψ ψ ψ ψ ψ ψ ψ ψ ψ ψ ψ ψ

The Devil Made Me Do It!

*I meticulously and systematically picked out all the chocolate chips
from a half-gallon container of chocolate chip ice cream.
And then I meticulously and systematically ate them.*

YOU are lost in Sin City and the food police have arrested you.

Cash in one of your Get Out of Jail Free cards or meticulously floss your teeth after every dietary transgression, removing all food remnants and reminders of chocolate in any way, shape, or form.

Get Out of Jail Free Card

The Sin City food police
have arrested you.

This card may be kept until
needed. It is nontransferable

All is forgiven, move on

DAYS-OF-THE-WEEK UNDERWEAR

I thought it would be fun to have days of the week underwear, but instead of having them say "Monday," "Tuesday," "Wednesday," I went with words that correlated with my cooking style of the day. I used regular panties, but tummy control are always an option!

Monday—Roasted
Tuesday—Fried
Wednesday—Baked
Thursday—Over Easy
Friday—Sautéed
Saturday—au Naturel
Sunday—Raw

225

STEP 92

EMOTIONAL EATER

"Give me a dozen heartbreaks . . . if you think it would help me lose one pound."
—Colette

think about something other than food

find your G spot

G

Garcia

ARE YOU AN EMOTIONAL EATER?

Food acts as a great defense against the stress in our lives. The only problem is that the relief you're feeling is short-lived. That piece of cake may have given you a couple of minutes of relief, but you will then have to deal with your feelings of guilt and shame for eating it. You have to approach emotional eating through awareness. Step back, observe, and find a way to reroute your upset.

An emotional eater is someone who uses food to manage his or her feelings, to self-soothe, to anesthetize. Some people call it compulsive overeating or food addiction. No matter the name, people use food because somewhere along the way, it worked.

Both eating and thinking about food serve as great diversions from being in touch with your uncomfortable feelings. Shifting your focus to food takes the edge off feelings of boredom,

226

stress, anxiety, anger, loneliness, happiness, fear, sadness, etc. Using food to manage your feelings becomes a self-reinforcing habit.

Having said that, emotional eating is normal. We celebrate with food. When something sad happens, family and friends bring food to our homes, taking care of us. However, when eating is our primary mood regulator and our primary coping mechanism, and is having a negative impact on the quality of our lives, we need to find a way to disconnect this food button and find more adaptive ways to feel better.

Svelte Talk

SEED—Something that is the source of a significant shift in perspective.

✳ NEW POINT OF VIEW

I now make a conscious effort to become aware of the ways in which I use food and have developed healthy coping strategies. I walk, breathe, and shift my focus from food to self-love and wellness. ✳

FORGIVERCISE
Planting Seeds

Start your day with a thought or quote or song that calms . . .

"You do not need to leave your room. Remain sitting at your table and listen. Do not even listen, simply wait. Do not even wait—be quiet, still and solitary. The world will freely offer itself to you to be unmasked. It has no choice. It will roll in ecstasy at your feet."—Franz Kafka

How nice to know that there is really nothing that I have to do. And now that I am in an open and relaxed station, I emotionally create my day. I hear myself laughing. I see others smiling. Feelings of happiness surface. I say smart things. Creativity flows.

How will you feel today? Plant your seeds and they will miraculously sprout, grow, and blossom!

FUEL STOP 93

ROCK STAR ROASTED FINGERLING FRIES

SERVINGS: 4

INGREDIENTS

16 fingerling potatoes, cut into halves
1 red onion, thinly sliced
2 teaspoons olive oil
1½ teaspoons kosher salt
½ teaspoon ground black pepper
½ teaspoon garlic powder
1 teaspoon dried thyme

INSTRUCTIONS

1. Preheat the oven to 400°F.
2. In a bowl, mix the potatoes, onions, and olive oil. Toss to combine them and sprinkle them with the salt, pepper, garlic powder, and thyme.
3. Pour the potato mixture into a large baking dish.
4. Roast the potatoes in the oven, stirring occasionally, for 40–45 minutes or until the potatoes are tender and golden.

Nutrition Facts		
Serving Size (210g)		
Servings Per Container 4		
Amount Per Serving		
Calories 200	Calories from Fat 25	
		% Daily Value*
Total Fat 2.5g		4%
Saturated Fat 0g		0%
Trans Fat 0g		
Cholesterol 0mg		0%
Sodium 890mg		37%
Total Carbohydrate 41g		14%
Dietary Fiber 5g		20%
Sugars 3g		
Protein 5g		
Vitamin A 0%	•	Vitamin C 40%
Calcium 4%	•	Iron 15%

*Percent Daily Values are based on a 2,000 calorie diet. Your daily values may be higher or lower depending on your calorie needs:

		Calories	2,000	2,500
Total Fat	Less Than		65g	80g
Saturated Fat	Less Than		20g	25g
Cholesterol	Less Than		300mg	300 mg
Sodium	Less Than		2,400mg	2,400mg
Total Carbohydrate			300g	375g
Dietary Fiber			25g	30g

Calories per gram:
Fat 9 • Carbohydrate 4 • Protein 4

S♆N C♆TY

♄ ♄ ♄ ♄ ♄ ♄ ♄ ♄ ♄ ♄ ♄ ♄ ♄ ♄ ♄ ♄ ♄

The Devil Made Me Do It!

*The evil demon estrogen took hold of my spirit and led me
straight down the road of bad food and overeating.
I now feel old AND fat! I kneel at your altar and
ask for forgiveness and for strength!
Cheers from your loyal convert in London—Karen*

YOU are lost in Sin City and the food police have arrested you.

Cash in one of your Get Out of Jail Free cards or go to directly to your
closest Betsey Johnson dress shop, buy a dress that is just a tad too young
for you, and go out on the town.

Get Out of Jail Free Card

The *Sin City* food police
have arrested you.

This card may be kept until
needed. It is nontransferable

All is forgiven, move on

YOUR AURA IS DIRTY

As seen on a bumper sticker:
"Out of body. Will be back in 15 minutes!"

creative
acts
of
weight
loss

Sometimes, as I travel the countryside, talking to folks, counseling about Permanent Fat Removal, they tell me things that I just have to pass along. Such was the case with Aurora. She contacted me because she wanted to lose about 15 pounds, in addition to the 15 pounds she had lost after having her aura cleaned.

I hadn't heard about aura cleaning . . . but I am most definitely open to new ways of weighing less, so I did a bit of research. Those of you with an open mind, please read on.

CLEAN YOUR AURA!

Think of your aura as an egg filled with energy, and imagine that you are the yolk of the egg. Your aura is like a magnet. It picks up vibrational energies that are floating everywhere you go.

It may prove helpful to cleanse your aura. And for you skeptics, it is at the very least a creative act of weight loss—by definition, that's anything you do that feels good, feeds your soul, and keeps you from eating (the "bad" stuff or in excess or when you're not hungry).

Let's cleanse our auras—and free them from foreign and negative energies. You'll feel energized, good about yourself, and centered. Hence, no need for food!

SEEING IS BELIEVING

You can see your aura. Simply go into the bathroom or bedroom and look into a mirror at night, under electric light. Relax, let your gaze soften, and as you look intently into your mirror image, you will, within ten minutes or so, see an outline of white light around your body. If you keep gazing, other colors may become apparent.

FEEL YOUR AURA

If the mirror didn't reveal your aura, don't worry. There are ways to feel it.

Sit in a comfortable chair with your feet firmly planted on the floor. Place your hands on your thighs, palms facing up. Take in a deep, cleansing breath. Imagine a beautiful white light pouring over your head and over your body. Imagine a waterfall cleansing the outside of your body as well as in the inside. Imagine

that your aura is being cleaned and the water is leaving you through the bottom of your feet, all the while breathing in and out, in and out.

You will start to feel calmer and cleaner! Here are a few other simple ways to do it.

1. Wash your hands. Using your fingers, comb through the space surrounding your body from head to toe. Wash your hands afterward. (Alternatively, ask someone else to do it for you.)
2. Take a shower.
3. Walk in the rain. (But—oh—not an electrical storm!)
4. Run like the wind into the wind.
5. Using a single feather, sweep through the space around your body.
6. Take an Epsom salt bath. (Always a great idea! Negative energies vanish in the steam.)

Svelte Talk **VIBRATOR—**An electric device that vibrates and, when held against the body, helps to generate good vibes that have a ripple effect, pulsating throughout the air.

❋ NEW POINT OF VIEW

I have an open mind, and I am willing, able, and ready to investigate new "weighs" of being and bathing! ❋

All Is Forgiven, Move On

231

"E" STOP 95

HULA HOOP YOUR "WEIGH" THIN

- In 1958, Hula Hoops cost $1.98 and one hundred million were sold worldwide.

- At the peak of their popularity, Wham-O manufactured twenty thousand Hula Hoops a day.

- The plastic tube used for all the Hula Hoops ever made would stretch around the earth more than five times.

Want to give yourself a great cardiovascular workout, increase your strength and flexibility, feel more agile, and have fun all at the same time?

Researchers have found that doing the Hula Hoop for a mere ten minutes is more effective than a fifteen-minute jog. Hula Hoop gets the energy flowing and the endorphins pumping, thereby improving your mental health.

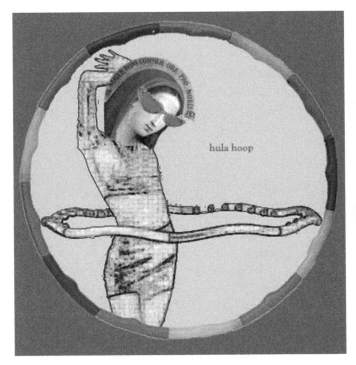

hula hoop

> Endorphins are a hormonelike substance that is produced by the brain and the pituitary gland. These magical opiates increase our tolerance for pain and create a state of happiness.

Using a Hula Hoop helps to:

Build abs while blasting fat from your belly;
Sculpt your thighs and arms—not to mention the awesome butt you're sure to have;
Stimulate your libido;
Relieve stress; and
Release endorphins, leaving you feeling happy and energized.

It is important to have the right size Hula Hoop. A general rule of thumb is that when you place the hoop standing up on the floor, it should reach somewhere between your stomach and nipple. The bigger you are, the bigger the hoop should be. Large hoops rotate more slowly and make getting started easier. Smaller hoops are more challenging but are great for tricks!

If you were to Hula Hoop for an entire hour, you'd burn off close to 800 calories! (As if! Ten minutes—a more doable goal—will burn off 133 calories.)

CAUTION: Fast turns ahead! Beginners sometimes hula or "turn" too fast, causing injuries to the joints and muscles. (But, compared to jogging, the incidence of injury is much lower.) There's no shock to the body when working out with your Hula Hoop. In jogging, a direct heel strike can lead to arthritis and degeneration in the knees, hips, and spine!

So, boys and girls, start out slow. Be sure to Hula Hoop in a clear space, warm up with a pleasant five-minute walk and do a bit of slow stretching.

(Source: HoopGirl.com)

 Svelte Talk

HULA-BALOO—Noisy excitement or fuss made over someone who swivels his or her hips in a lively, enthusiastic manner.

❋ NEW POINT OF VIEW

I can swivel my hips and Hula Hoop my way thin! ❋

HAWAIIAN HULA PUNCH

SERVINGS: 8

INGREDIENTS

- 2 medium bananas, cut into chunks
- 1 ripe mango, cut into chunks
- 1 ripe papaya, cut into chunks
- 4 cups unsweetened pineapple juice
- 4 cups seltzer

INSTRUCTIONS

In a blender, mix the bananas, mango, papaya, and pineapple juice. Puree until the mixture is smooth, and pour it into individual glasses, filling each one halfway. Add the seltzer, and serve.

Nutrition Facts		
Serving Size (337g)		
Servings Per Container 8		
Amount Per Serving		
Calories 130	Calories from Fat 5	
		% Daily Value*
Total Fat 0g		0%
Saturated Fat 0g		0%
Trans Fat 0g		
Cholesterol 0mg		0%
Sodium 0mg		0%
Total Carbohydrate 32g		11%
Dietary Fiber 2g		8%
Sugars 23g		
Protein 1g		
Vitamin A 20%	•	Vitamin C 100%
Calcium 4%	•	Iron 2%

*Percent Daily Values are based on a 2,000 calorie diet. Your daily values may be higher or lower depending on your calorie needs:

		Calories	2,000	2,500
Total Fat	Less Than		65g	80g
Saturated Fat	Less Than		20g	25g
Cholesterol	Less Than		300mg	300 mg
Sodium	Less Than		2,400mg	2,400mg
Total Carbohydrate			300g	375g
Dietary Fiber			25g	30g

Calories per gram:
Fat 9 • Carbohydrate 4 • Protein 4

STEP 97

NO WAY! YOU'RE NOT TAKING THAT AWAY FROM ME!

OR, YOU CAN HAVE YOUR TREAT AND EAT IT, TOO!

WEAR YOUR CHOCOLATE CHIPS WITH PANACHE

"Stressed spelled backwards is desserts.
Coincidence? I think not!"
—*Author Unknown*

Here we are, step #97, and perhaps you're beginning to want a piece of chocolate or some other goodie that you may have thought was completely off limits, vanished from your life forever. Oh, how sad.

Well, cheer up! I've got some good news for you: Nothing is off limits. You can have your treat and eat it too! You don't have to permanently give up those foods that you love. This is Permanent Fat Removal, not permanent deprivation!

You just have to figure out how to make your favorite foods a part of your plan and/or find substitutions that really cut it—and that are just as satisfying. (Stop rolling your eyes!

chocolate chip chiffon

chocolate chip chiffon

235

Baked potato chips are even better than French fries.)

I have a few favorites myself: chocolate, coffee, wine, and mayo. You may have guessed the first three, but mayo? Why mayo, you ask?

Mayo is a favorite for sentimental reasons. When I was four years old, my neighbor taught me how to make a mayonnaise sandwich. It was my very first culinary masterpiece.

I queried a gaggle of Our Lady of Weight Loss's Kick in the Tush Club members, wondering what they just won't give up. Would what you all don't want to give up be the same list as what I don't want to give up? No way! You guys are far more inventive than I! Here's what y'all had to say!

Svelte Talk

LEGAL HOLIDAY—A day established as a holiday under the Laws of Permanent Fat Removal, when one is invited to put down one's counting machine and ingest as much chocolate as one desires. There are three such holidays on record: Valentine's Day, Your Birthday, and New Year's Eve (last chance before your resolution kicks in).

❋ NEW POINT OF VIEW

One ounce of chocolate a day keeps the devil away! ❋

"NO WAY! YOU ARE NOT TAKING THAT AWAY!"

Coffee (with cream and sugar) • Wine • Pasta • Alcohol • Chocolate • Peanut Butter • French Fries • Popcorn at the Movies • Hot Dogs • Raisins (I know they're high in sugar, but I love 'em on everything!) • Beer (I am a beer snob and have a beer cellar instead of a wine cellar.) • Chicken-Fried Steak (with cream gravy) • Ramen Noodles (Deceptively high in calories. I looked one day—goodness gracious, I nearly fell over, but I'm not givin' up!) • Real Peanut Butter • Wonder White Bread (Sorry, but it's true.) • Butter • Bacon, Egg, and Cheese Sandwiches • Lava Cake • McDonald's French Fries • Chocolate Cake with Buttercream Frosting • Scotch on the Rocks • Scotch in My Egg Nog • Scotch in My Coffee & Tea • Scotch, Plain and Simple • Peanut Butter and Banana Sandwiches • Peanut Butter and Jelly Sandwiches • Peanut Butter on Crackers • Spoonfuls of Peanut Butter • Rum Balls • Sno Balls • Ribbon Candy • Cheese (full-fat, part-skim, 2% fat-free—any and all cheese) • Coney Island Hot Dogs with an Egg Cream • Fox's u-bet • Half & Half

creative curves ahead

My friend Christina Stahr is a chocoholic. She indulges in one piece of truly expensive, high-end, mouth-watering chocolate per day.

She feels that there's just no point in eating the cheap stuff. She's got style! And she recycles the wrappers from the chocolate and creates the most amazing collages. Check out her "Chocolate Obsession Collages" at www.christinastahr.com.

I agree wholeheartedly with Christina. Treat yourself to the absolute best, most expensive chocolate you can find. If it's expensive enough, you won't be able to afford more than one piece a day. And read the labels. Look for single-bean chocolates with about 70 percent cocoa content.

S✝N C✝TY

✝ ✝ ✝ ✝ ✝ ✝ ✝ ✝ ✝ ✝ ✝ ✝ ✝ ✝ ✝

The Devil Made Me Do It!

I cannot give it up. I'm hooked . . .
have to have a piece each and every day.
Sometimes more (but never less) . . .
When the PMS kicks in, forgetaboutit.

YOU are lost in Sin City and the food police have arrested you.

Cash in one of your Get Out of Jail Free cards or buy a kitchen scale and measure one ounce of chocolate (and that's it!) or chocolate privileges will be taken away from you for one month!

Get Out of Jail Free Card

The Sin City food police have arrested you.

This card may be kept until needed. It is nontransferable

All is forgiven, move on

STEP 98

YOU HAVE ARRIVED . . .
WELCOME TO SVELTESVILLE

"Love is the greatest refreshment in life."
—Pablo Picasso

CONGRATULATIONS! YOU'VE ARRIVED

That's right. You've arrived at a new place of understanding, a new way of being. You've had a journey filled with high-wattage-lightbulb moments, creative curves, plenty of laughs, some tears, red-carpet moments, and word games!

YOU ARE SERIOUS ABOUT
PERMANENT FAT REMOVAL, BUT NOT HEAVY!

You are filled with confidence and sure of yourself because you have taken these enormous first steps. You've come to realize that the real goal is simply to be the best that you can be and to love yourself first and foremost. You are eternally optimistic and filled with possibility.

Permanent Fat Removal is as much about self-love as it is about weight loss. They go hand in hand, or thigh to thigh, if you will.

Loving yourself is a skill that requires conviction and daily practice. It's there within you, always available to comfort and embrace. You only have nice things to say to yourself. You are filled with praise. You deserve to love yourself.

❋ NEW POINT OF VIEW

I appreciate, admire, accept, and love myself—and it feels oh, so good! ❋

Svelte Talk   **LOVE AFFAIR**—Finding oneself absolutely irresistible—so irresistible that one dresses up, gussies up, and sneaks off with oneself on secret dates.

CHOCOLATE BANANA ROYAL FLUSH

N O doubt you are thirsty. It's been quite a journey!
Bottoms up, everyone! Enjoy.

SERVINGS: 1

INGREDIENTS

1 medium banana
5 chocolate chips, dark chocolate
1 tablespoon slivered almonds, toasted
1 teaspoon cocoa powder

INSTRUCTIONS

1. Preheat the oven to 400°F.
2. With the help of a paring knife, carefully open the middle part of the banana peel, making sure the top and bottom are left intact. Press slightly to open the banana. Make five incisions. Place the banana on a piece of foil.
3. Press the chocolate chips into the incisions and top them with almonds
4. Dust the banana with the cocoa powder and close the foil around the banana, making a small package.
5. Bake the banana in the oven for 15–20 minutes.

Nutrition Facts		
Serving Size (128g)		
Servings Per Container 1		
Amount Per Serving		
Calories 150		Calories from Fat 40
		% Daily Value*
Total Fat 4.5g		7%
Saturated Fat 1g		5%
Trans Fat 0g		
Cholesterol 0mg		0%
Sodium 0mg		0%
Total Carbohydrate 31g		10%
Dietary Fiber 5g		20%
Sugars 16g		
Protein 3g		
Vitamin A 2%	•	Vitamin C 15%
Calcium 2%	•	Iron 4%

*Percent Daily Values are based on a 2,000 calorie diet. Your daily values may be higher or lower depending on your calorie needs:

	Calories	2,000	2,500
Total Fat	Less Than	65g	80g
Saturated Fat	Less Than	20g	25g
Cholesterol	Less Than	300mg	300 mg
Sodium	Less Than	2,400mg	2,400mg
Total Carbohydrate		300g	375g
Dietary Fiber		25g	30g

Calories per gram:
Fat 9 • Carbohydrate 4 • Protein 4

STEP 100

SVELTESVILLE WALK OF FAME

EX-FATTY SECTION, JUST EAST
OF HOLLYWOOD BOULEVARD

Some stars are 600,000 times as bright as our sun.

OWN YOUR POWER.
BE THE STAR THAT YOU ARE.

Be proud, be happy, and get that red-carpet dress (the one you wore when you received your Ph.D. in dieting at the beginning of your journey), have the dressed altered, trimmed in leopard, perhaps—or not—whatever you feel to be befitting for the new you!

We are headed to the Sveltesville Walk of Fame to sign our names to our stars, next to those other fabulous and famous ex-fatties' . . . Kirstie Alley, Valerie Bertinelli, and Oprah. (Who else can you think of?)

Remember, we are most powerful when we are our authentic selves, when we are operating from a place of integrity, when we have a vision and are actively pursuing our goals. For without a sense of where we are going, we might easily get lost.

- Believe in yourself.
- Let your uniqueness show; fly your freak flag!
- Do what pleases you.
- Honor your core values.
- Don't let your limitations get in your way.
- Make requests of others.
- Never play the victim.
- Be open to the possibilities.
- Risk more.

Our Lady of Weight Loss is 100 percent sure that you are a star. Feel confident in your stardom. Flaunt it, baby! It's not only okay to own it—it's the right thing to do!

Svelte STAR—YOU! Talk

✳ NEW POINT OF VIEW

I shine through and through. ✳

SVELTESVILLE'S NATIONAL ANTHEM: AMAZING WEIGHT

The Our Lady of Weight-Loss Cheerleaders present
Sveltesville's National Anthem: Amazing Weight
(to be sung to the tune of "Amazing Grace")
(to be sung immediately after star signing)

Amazing weight (how sweet the feel)
Of bones beneath my skin
I once was fat but now I'm slim
My thinner core set free.

'Twas weight that was a-holding me back
And weight coverin' my fears
How precious when weight disappeared
The hour I first believed.

Through my biscuits, fries, and cakes, mmmmmmmmmm
I did come to see
That now it's time for me to stop
Using foods to comfort me.

Our Lady has promised good to me
Her words my hope secure
As I weigh and measure my portions be
As long as life endures.

Yes, my flesh and heart do sing of vitality
My life is flying high you see
As I possess a thinner me
For all the world to see.

The fat cells are dissolving now
I slip and slide in these
But Our Lady, who called me here
Says I am forever free.

Janice
Taylor

246

ABOUT THE AUTHOR
An Early Oral History

In answer to one of the most-asked questions ("Did you always have a weight problem?")... Like, HELLO, I was born fat!

BORN FAT!

Most babies lose an ounce or two their first week on the planet, but not me. I was the only baby in the hospital nursery to gain weight. An ominous sign!

My parents were enormously proud. They told all who would listen, "She gained! Her first week! A genius! She sucks like no other." The fat jokes were the only thing about me that wore thin.

By the time I reached second grade, I weighed 112 pounds.

The good news was that my best friend, Barbara R., weighed 113 pounds. She was the fat one!

Still, the kids were mercilessly mean, as kids are wont to be, and chanted each and every morning, as I approached the bus stop, "Here comes Fatty Lu."

I ignored them best I could. My name was not Fatty Lu!

HELLO
my name is

NOT FATTY LU

Janice
Taylor

SOMEBODY SAVE ME, PLEASE

I wanted to escape it all, and I found great relief in writing letters to Hollywood producers, in hopes that I would be "discovered"—"saved." It was the first of my letter writing campaigns.

> *Dear Mr. Producer,*
>
> *I am a chubby and interesting-looking eight-year-old girl. I have dark hair, dark eyes, and an olive complexion. People ask me if I am adopted and wonder if I am from India. I am not.*
>
> *Oh, and I wear light blue "cat-eye" glasses with gold flecks.*
>
> *I have a lot of character. Do you need a child actor like me in Hollywood? Please come and discover me.*
>
> *Janice*

Sadly, I had no stamps or addresses, but I believed that the United States Postal Service

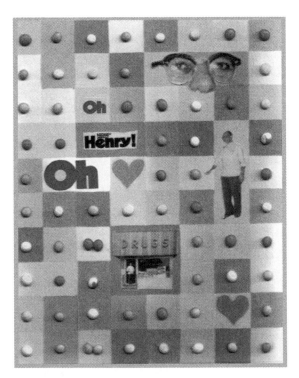

surely knew the specific addresses and would kindly deliver my letters.

At the same time, I "found" the nuns at the Convent of Our Lady of the Snows. They offered a different form of discovery and salvation than Hollywood. Their salvation came in the form of kindness!

My dad owned a pharmacy, and my mother and I would make deliveries to the nuns.

The nuns were always kind and sweet, and unlike the rest of the town (population 2,500), they never made mention of my fat state. They told me that I was good. A good girl for accompanying my mother on deliveries; a good girl for selling Girl Scout cookies with such commitment (they were my best customers); a good girl for praying, believing, and just being.

I prayed "Please [I was always polite] may I wake up 'naturally' thin."

I also prayed for white go-go boots. Oh, how I wanted to be a dancer on Shindig, a popular variety show.

I cast my salvation net wide and far. Toward the west—Hollywood; and towards the east—the church. Who might answer my prayers? (David O. Selznick or Mother Teresa?)

go
go-girl

HOME AT THE RANCH

Back at the homestead, as all mothers pass along their truths to their daughters, Mother passed along her happy home philosophy to me.

One must always color coordinate one's dinners. "It would be very boring," she told me, "to have all beige foods on the plate." True, true, true, I must admit!

"Fresh baked goods make a house smell like a home." Interesting point. Although I've realized in recent years, that a great-smelling, low-cal turkey chili could fit the bill. But okay, Mom! Thanks.

"Life is nothing without dessert." The names

Sara Lee and Betty Crocker were bandied about at home with such frequency that I began to think of them as family members. Would Aunt Betty be joining us for dinner? More than likely, yes!

Mother insisted, "It's improper to cut slices of cake in an uneven manner. Should you inadvertently cut yourself a slice that isn't entirely straight and neat, you must try again and make it 'even.'" We would sometimes polish off an entire cake "evening it out." She was sure that there were no calories in jagged pieces of cake. An out 'n' out lie. Sorry, Mom! (I do love you, though. Don't worry. As it turns out, you've given me so much to write about!)

And last, but certainly not least, were the weekly visits to the local Entenmann's Outlet, where we would pick up day-old or "cracked" cake (cake that had been dropped and looked like a minor earthcake had hit it! Oh dear—a Freudian slice; I meant earthquake, not earthcake! And yes, I meant slip, not slice. Oops.) We would buy a minimum of seven cakes.

THE BERMUDA TRIANGLE OF MY CHILDHOOD— MOTHER, CONVENT, MAILBOX

And so it went: Time spent with my mother and my faux aunts, Sara Lee and Betty Crocker, the kindly nuns at the Convent of Our Lady of the Snows, the walks to the mailbox and my imaginary musings with Hollywood producers, who would ultimately save me (my version of the knight on the white horse?) and cast me as a "child character actor."

DON'T CRY FOR ME!

Decades passed, and truthfully, nobody came to my rescue. (Pass the Kleenex. Sob! Sob!)

I yo-yoed here and there, tried a gazillion diets, lost fat, found it all plus some—until Our Lady of Weight Loss entered my life. And the rest, as they say, is history—or in this case . . . HERstory!

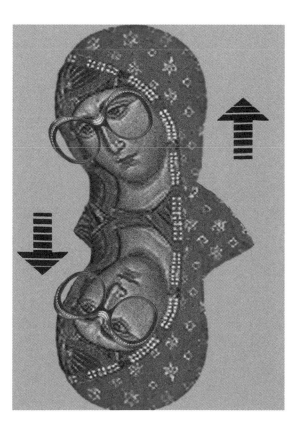

ANSWERS TO QUIZZES

Answers to Test Your Food Vocabulary (page 17)

1. Dibble: To drink like a duck, lifting up the head after each sip
2. Groak: To watch people silently while they are eating, hoping they will ask you to join them
3. Gynotikolobomassophile: One who likes to nibble on a woman's earlobes
4. Libberwort: Food or drink that makes one idle and stupid, food of no nutritional value, i.e., junk food
5. Pilgarlic: A bald head that looks like a peeled garlic
6. Chanking: Spat-out food (rinds or pits)
7. Farctate: The state of being overstuffed with food (overeating)
8. Lachanophobia: The fear of vegetables
9. Ruminant: Cud chewer

Answers to Fruit or Veggie Quiz (page 52)

To know whether a tomato is a fruit or vegetable, you first need to know what makes a fruit a fruit and a vegetable a vegetable. It's all in the seeds! If the food in question has seeds, then technically, it's a fruit.

Therefore, tomatoes, cucumbers, squash, green beans, and walnuts are fruits. Radishes, celery, carrots, and lettuce are vegetables.

Answers to Word Jumble (page 112)

MARINADE
CHOCOLATE
WATERCRESS

Answers to Fill-in-the-Name Game
(page 138)

Sloppy JOE
Eggs BENEDICT
Hamburger PATTY
Beef WELLINGTON
Apple Brown BETTY
Cuppa' JOE
Quiche LORRAINE
Peach MELBA
Oh! HENRY

All Is
Forgiven,
Move On

KICK IN THE TUSH CLUB CHAPTERS
A Miracle

Kick in the Tush Club is Our Lady of Weight Loss's online group, created for those of us who want to chit the chat, dish the dirt, steam some veggies, and melt the fat! You can join the group (It's free! Woo hoo!) just by going to www.ourladyofweightloss.com and signing up! You can also form your own chapters.

After Hurricane Katrina, I received an e-mail from a minister at a church in Belle Chasse, Louisiana. Reverend Duke wondered if it would be okay if she started a Kick in the Tush Club chapter in her church. Seems they wanted to bring some normalcy and fun back into their lives. I was honored. Of course they could start a Kick in the Tush Club Chapter.

Similarly, a group of women in Tomahawk, Wisconsin, said that the economy had given them a kick in the tush of a not-so-pleasant nature, and they were looking to lift their spirits,

celebrate something. They asked if they could start a Kick in the Tush Club Chapter, too!

Since that time, Kick in the Tush Club chapters have been popping up all across the country. It's so important to have Permanent Fat Removal support. Friends, family, and townspeople have formed groups, some meeting weekly, some biweekly, some monthly, and some virtually.

They have given themselves some tush-kickin' names and deeply meaningful missions:

The Flush Flush Club: If you ain't a-peein', the fat ain't a-fleein' (Mission: to drink a lot of water and pee a lot)
LOPA (Ladies of Perpetual Atonement) (Mission: to have fun, fun, fun while they forgive themselves for their sinful dietary transgressions)

If you'd like to start your own chapter, please feel free to do so. It's all about lightening up in any way you can think of!

You can register either by going to my Web site (www.ourladyofweightloss.com) and clicking on "start your own Kick in the Tush Club chapter" or by filling out the form at the end of this book and mailing or e-mailing it to me!

HOW TO START YOUR OWN KICK IN THE TUSH CLUB CHAPTER

Gather your family, friends, or work buddies and start your own chapter.

Swap (low-fat, low-cal, healthy—please) righteous recipes. Or chew the fat, dish the dirt, confess your weighty sins (and then immediately move on). Meet weekly, biweekly, or monthly. Meet in person or virtually.

There are no rules. Well maybe one . . . that you take the Kick in the Tush Club Oath and smile when doing so!

If you do start your own chapter, I sure would like to know about it. There's a form below for you to fill out and either mail or cut, paste, and e-mail to me (janice@kickinthetush club.com). This way I can let you know when special things are happening and keep you in the Kick in the Tush Club inner-circle loop!

Name of your chapter:
Kick in the Tush Club: _____ Chapter.
Your Leading Lady (you know, who's in charge?)

_____

Address: _____

Phone number: _____

E-mail address: _____

How often do you plan to meet? (weekly, monthly?) _____

What are your goals? How can Our Lady of Weight Loss help you?

_____

Members' information: (As many or as few members as you like.)
Name / Address / E-mail address (for weekly KICK!)

E-mail to: janice@kickinthetushclub.com   Feel free to send your questions and
or mail to: comments.
Janice Taylor   Our Lady is always happy to
KICK IN THE TUSH CLUB   hear from you.
Morningside Station
P.O. Box 1674   info@OurLadyofWeightLoss.com
NY, NY 10026